JESUS IS STILL JESUS

DENNIS FUNDERBURG

 FIVE CROWNS

Praise for Dennis Funderburg

"There are many beautiful Jesus lovers who will be forerunners for the greatest harvest the earth has ever seen, and I believe Dennis and the Five Crowns team are among that group! These champions of the faith will lead with pure hearts and the deepest passion to see souls encounter Jesus. Spend five minutes with this ministry and you will experience it, and they are just beginning!"

Gabriel Jackson - United Hive

"Five Crowns spearheads the mission of bringing souls to Jesus. With Holy prudence, Evangelist Dennis and his team lead the way in equipping Churches which is instrumental in ensuring discipleship for those who made their decision to live for Jesus."

Bryant Borges, M.A. - QMHP Founder and Author of The Face Of Jesus

"Five Crowns is making a difference! The message you bring is changing lives. In the midst of so many distractions thank you for refocusing our attention to the reality that JESUS is Still JESUS! Your topics are so relevant and so real. Thank you for sharing your life, ministry & experiences. Just like John the Baptist, a Voice and you have a Message for today's generation. Blessed to know you and learn from you. Glory to God!"

Nelrose Sasam - ROLFC in Davao City, Philippines

Contents

ONE

I Didn't Know

*Remember not the former things, nor consider
the things of old. Behold, I am doing a new
thing; now it springs forth, do you not
perceive it? I will make a way in the
wilderness and rivers in the desert.*
Isaiah 43:18:19

I GREW up in a small Texas town of about five thousand people. I had said the prayer of salvation at the age of ten or so when I saw a play about people dying and either going to Heaven with Jesus or being taken by the devil and thrown into a pit. It terrified me so much that I guess you could say it 'scared the hell out of me.' The last thing I wanted that night was to end up in a place like Hell. I was so scared I couldn't stop shaking and crying. My prayer was a plea to Jesus to not punish me and send me to Hell. On that night I made Jesus my Savior, He was my 'get out of Hell' free card, but I did not understand Jesus as Lord. That didn't take place until much later in my life. In between those two times I went to church a handful of times, I would attempt to read the Bible every once and awhile, and I tried to make sure my good deeds outweighed the bad. I didn't know. I thought Jesus paid the price to get me into Heaven, but it was on my shoulders to live a 'good' life and for me to make something of myself. There were times I would pray, "God, let me have a good day today." Or "God, I know you are really busy, so I won't bother you. Life is going Ok, I'll let you know if I need something. Please tell everyone in Heaven I said Hi."

There were times in my young life when family members would get sick. I remember I would get away to be alone and I would pray to God asking Him, "God, please take that sickness off of them and give it to me if you have to." Thankfully, He never did do that, but I didn't know. I didn't know about the real love that Jesus has for us. I didn't know that Jesus didn't just die and resurrect to get us into Heaven, but He died and resurrected to get Heaven into us. I didn't know He could heal people from sickness and disease. I didn't know Jesus could set people free of mental torment or spiritual oppression. I didn't know the Holy Spirit wanted to fill me with His love and power. I didn't know.

I also didn't know what the world had to say about Jesus. I thought everyone believed in Jesus. I didn't know about all the theological debates between the conservative and charismatic church that has been bellowing for generations. I didn't know the devil was really trying to steal, kill, and destroy me and everything I had. I didn't know people would disagree on what God 'does' do and what He "doesn't do" anymore. I didn't know people spoke and prayed in tongues or the clash of belief that came with it. I didn't know about people using their spiritual gifts for personal gain. I didn't know people wanted their comfort more than they wanted a move of God. I was just a Texas boy doing his absolute best to live a 'good' life, but even at that, I was failing miserably.

In 2011, I was a 26-year-old martial arts instructor. My high school sweetheart and I had been married for two years up to that point. I would work out all day and teach classes in the evening. I idolized the traditions and the sport of martial arts. I was a very stern instructor and expected perfection out of myself and my students. I always put on a happy face when people were around. I would laugh and joke around with everyone, but when I was alone...that was when problems came to the surface. I was having a major identity crisis. Nothing I did seemed to give me fulfillment. I had many people comment about my size and stature and I allowed that to penetrate my heart. I was haunted by words on repeat in my head, "You're not good enough. You're not strong enough. You're weak and pathetic. You can't do anything right. Your life means nothing. Nobody loves you. You are a huge disappointment. It would be better for everyone if you were not here anymore."

I would have the most awful nightmares at night. I would constantly dream of these dark shadows chasing me and tormenting me. I would wake up in the middle of the night in terror because I would see the shadows in my dreams moving around my bedroom at night. I was hooked on pornography. I bought into the lie that "all men do it." I couldn't stand the person I saw in the mirror. There was one time I cursed myself out in the mirror for over 20 minutes telling myself how worthless I was. (You will hear more about this in a later chapter.) I was self-medicating with pain killers, and I kept myself in isolation. After all, who on earth could I tell these things to? No one would understand, or so I thought. I was isolated, disappointed, and ashamed of my life, actions, and struggles. I didn't want to live anymore.

At my school I started having problems. Every time I would walk into my own school, I would get the worst stomach ache and the sense of absolute dread. I kept the school as clean as I possibly could and had an infestation of flies. I literally killed more than two hundred flies in one day. There were two occasions when I heard an audible verse speak to me. The first time I was working on the heavy bag. I had 3-pound weighted wrist wraps with 18-ounce boxing gloves on. I would hit the bag for five minutes at a time or until I couldn't hold my arms up. I was driven by self-hatred and I would literally torture myself every day in attempt to feel better. While I was hitting the bag, I heard a voice say, "Smash your head into the bag until you die." It startled me. I turned around sharply to see who said it. There wasn't a single soul in the five thousand square foot school. I felt so sick to my stomach after that I wanted to vomit. The second time I was working out on a cable machine when the voice returned saying, "Hang yourself." I jumped up from the machine and yelled, "Where are you? Who's saying that?" Was I losing my mind? Why was this happening to me? I couldn't understand what was going on and my business that once had one hundred and fifty clients had dwindled down to forty. I was falling apart and so was my business.

One day at the school I was approached by one of the parents of my students who was also a pastor. He grabbed me by the arm and sternly said, "We need to talk, now." We shuffled to my office and shut the door. I asked him if everything was ok and with a concerned look on his face he said, "Dennis, something is not right in this building. I really think you may have a demon in this school." I was shocked by his statement, but a part of me believed him. It was as if all the dots finally connected to why I was feeling what I was feeling and struggling with what I was struggling with.

I began to tell him how I had been feeling and what I was going through.

He then gave me clear instructions to not confront it and that I was not strong enough to handle what was lurking in my school. That scared me even more. I didn't know what to do and I definitely didn't know what this 'devil' was going to do to me. Was it going to jump out and grab me? Can I kill it with a sword? Do I need to order some Holy water I've seen before on television and drench the place? What on earth do I do with this thing?

I decided to drive out to my parents' house and visit with my dad. My dad was also my martial art instructor and I heavily relied on him when it came to the school. I'll never forget that night. I walked into the house and my dad was laying on the couch watching tv in his pajamas. We did the normal small talk and I finally said, "Dad, I think I might have a problem at the school?" My dad's gaze changed, and He asked, "What kind of problem?" I was silent for a moment thinking I shouldn't have said anything at all, but I finally blurted it out, "A pastor told me I have a devil in the school, and I don't know what to do."

My dad had a long stare for a moment and then rose from the couch. "Ok." He said, "I'll be right back." My dad walked up the stairs to his room and came back down minutes later fully dressed with a Bible in his hands. "What are you doing dad?" I asked. "Son, that thing in your school doesn't belong there. We are going to go kick it out." I was even more terrified. "Dad, we can't. The pastor told me not to confront it. I don't even know how to confront something like this or if there is something really there. How can we fight something we can't even see?" My dad was done with discussion. He told me to get in the car and drive him to the school. Reluctantly I did.

We made the long drive to the school and a million thoughts

are running through my head. Is this really happening? I didn't think demons were actually real. Are we really about to see something? Experience something? Is this thing going to kill me? Am I saved? Is God mad at me? This list of questions and doubts were flashing a million miles an hour through my mind. I was scared. I looked over at my dad and I saw a calmness in his eyes. "Dad, do you have a plan?" I asked him as I saw the leather-bound Bible sitting on his lap. My dad replied, "Dennis, God made us to be warriors. When I was involved in the Church, I was trained by my pastor to handle these kinds of things." My dad then went on to tell me about how he grew quickly in the church but then got hurt by some of the leaders over political things and he refrained from leading ever since. The political games in the church caused my dad to withdraw and it prevented him from continuing to excel at that time.

We finally pulled up to the martial arts school. My dad got out of the car and he instructed me to unlock the door and let him walk in first. I did not protest him walking in first. My dad walked into the school with a very broad posture. He looked around the school and then moved over to a portion of the school that always gave me a very uncomfortable feeling. My dad knelt to the ground and opened up his Bible. I wish I could tell you what verses he was reading, but I cannot remember. After he had finished reading scripture out loud, he began praying. I was not prepared for what was about to happen. Again, I didn't know anything.

While my dad was praying, I slowly approached him to stand next to him. Suddenly the atmosphere in the room changed. A strong sense of dread and heaviness engulfed the room. My stomach began to hurt even more and then I heard it. My dad and I both heard a sound he or I could not replicate. It was a mix between a howl and a screech. I instantly had goosebumps all over my body. The walls in the building started making sounds as if the frame inside the walls were twisting. My dad continued to pray, and I started to as well. I didn't have a clue what to pray so I just started asking God to make whatever this thing was, to go away forever. As my dad and I prayed out loud I began to see the familiar shadow that I would see in my dreams and at night in bed. It was moving. The figure made more noises and moved away from us. Apparently, it didn't like what we were saying.

I suddenly felt something different as the figure moved away. I felt a type of calm peace settle on me that made me bolder. My dad and I both stepped closer to it and prayed even more. I remember repenting out loud to Jesus, confessing the porn and the pills. The "shadow" ended up relocating to the opposite corner of the room we were standing in. My dad and I were both holding hands and were covering the entry point of this room. The moment was very tense, and I remember saying, "Get out now and don't come back!" Immediately after I said it the shadow vanished, and I felt something hit my shoulder. I quickly looked at my dad because I thought he hit me. To my surprise my dad was looking at me with a very puzzled look on his face. He felt something hit him as well and he thought I hit him. While we were staring at each other the front door of the school swung wide open. It swung open so violently that it almost shattered. I thought to myself, "Did that devil just run between my dad and I, physically bump into us, and run out the building?" Silently my dad and I stared at the door as it closed softly on its own and suddenly something beautiful happened. The entire atmosphere of the school changed. There was an overwhelming sense of peace I had never felt before in my life. The peace was so strong in the room that it brought me to tears. Did that really just happen? Did we just cast out a devil? What is going on? My dad gave me a hug and told me everything was going to be ok.

I dropped my dad off at his house and began my hour-long drive to my apartment in Stephenville, Texas. What was I going to tell my wife? How would I explain something like this to her? We never talk about stuff like this. Is that "thing" going to come back? Is it going to follow me home? That car ride home I kept thinking of all the different things that happened; The dread, the stomach pains, the flies, what the pastor said, the sounds, the "shadow", and the fact that a heavy door swung wide open as we commanded a devil to leave. (The door was intentionally tightened and hard to open so young students couldn't open it on their own because the main street was close, and I didn't want them to get hit by a car.) Was all of this a coincidence? What was going to happen next in my life? My thoughts were racing. I wish I could tell you this was my big conversion moment and this story ends with a happily ever after. This was only the beginning of what was to unfold in 2011.

The next few weeks were chaotic. I had more questions and not enough answers. My business was free from demonic oppression, but my heart was still in trouble. As a matter of fact, I struggled even more. I had never encountered anything like that in my life and I was afraid it was only going to get worse. The conflict in my own thoughts got even darker. I didn't say anything to my wife, Miranda. I was having even more nightmares, this time, they were not "'shadows" anymore. They were like ruthless disfigured monsters that I could never escape from. I just knew it was only a matter of time these things were going to finish me off or I was going to do something to myself. The month of October of 2011 came, and I knew my life was at a huge crossroads. It was either going to be death or life.

It was the night of October 6th and my wife had just gone to bed at her usual time. She is a schoolteacher and had to wake up early every morning. Usually, every night after she would go to bed, my world became under siege and plagued by darkness and fear, but on that night, I felt something different. It was like I heard a voice inside me tell me to do something. I sat down at our dining room table and opened up my laptop. I went through my iTunes account and started deleting all of my music. I was so sick of hearing the same old lustful, prideful, arrogant, and angry music that I had submitted myself to for so long. I deleted ALL of them, over twelve hundred songs. I closed my eyes and out loud prayed, "God, if you're real, I need you to show up or say something. I'm at the end of myself." After I did that, I started randomly purchasing Christian music albums. I spent over eighty dollars that night. I sat there for hours listening to this new music that I could not understand. I even tried listening to different podcasts of some preachers a friend told me about. I listened and waited but heard nothing.

I shut down my laptop and murmured, "Maybe tomorrow." I shut off all the lights and walked down the hallway. I reached for the doorknob that led to my bedroom when I felt something. I felt the same type of peace I felt at the martial arts school when the demon ran out. I paused with my hand on the doorknob when I heard a voice. To be honest with you I'm not sure if the voice was audible or not. If it wasn't, it was so loud in my heart it might as well have been. This new, beautiful, and gentle voice said, "Son, turn around and go back to the table." I remained there for what seemed minutes. This voice was so different from all the others. It was calm but yet shook me. It was powerful and loving. It was gentle but made a raging river sound like a trickling fossette. What should I do? Is this.... God? Does He really speak? Am I losing my mind? I finally determined that I had nothing to lose by listening to this 'stranger.' It's funny looking back now that for years I professed to be a Christian but never knew the flow of His voice until that night. Sadly, this is also true for many other Christians in the world, but that is what this book is for. This book is to introduce us to the relational side of God, so we don't go another day without receiving what all Jesus paid for us to have.

I walked back to the small table and sat down, "What do you want me to do?" I asked out loud as I thought to myself, 'If I'm going to go for it, let's really go for it.' I paused, listened, and the voice returned, "Son, I know you love music... play some." I opened up my laptop once again and started playing this new Christian music I had downloaded hours earlier. I tried hard to listen to the lyrics of each song as if I were trying to decipher a great mystery. About three songs in something shifted. A song came on with lyrics that went like this, "Been fighting things that I can't see, like voices coming from inside of me. Like doing things I find hard to believe in. Am I myself or am I dreaming?" The song continued talking about the conflict of the person they saw in the mirror. At that moment my heart absolutely shattered. I became totally broken beyond repair. I sat there sobbing feeling as if all my guilt and shame was on display before me. I saw myself for what I was. I was a scared boy that didn't know the meaning of my life and helpless to the war waging inside and around me.

I was only in that condition for just a few moments when the entire atmosphere of the apartment changed. I wish I had the words to articulate what I felt at that moment, but the only way I know how to describe it is that royalty walked into the room. My focus left my hurts and pains and I became aware that I was not alone in the room. There was a presence in my apartment that shook the core of my soul. HE walked into the room. I couldn't see

Him, but I felt Him. It was Jesus. It was as if time stood still. There was a warm electricity in the air and everything became silent. The Savior of the world was standing next to me. The sensation was so overwhelming, and I was terrified to look up. I bowed my head low and closed my eyes. Jesus spoke again and this time I sensed emotions in His voice. It was as if He was crying with me. "Son, are you sick of this yet?" I immediately threw my hands up in the air and said, "Yes Jesus. I am so tired of the hurt and the pain. I don't know what to do. I'm sorry for all the times I have sinned and took you for granted. Jesus, I GIVE YOU EVERY-THING THAT I AM!"

At that moment I was a young man with nothing to lose and nothing to give. I was at a place of full surrender. I sat there with tears in my eyes as if I was waiting for a verdict from the creator of all things. Suddenly, I felt the presence get even stronger and I felt something touch my chest. It felt like someone put their hand on my chest. He was so close it was as if I could feel Him breathing on me. The pressure of the hand on my chest was gentle but powerful and I heard Him say, "It is finished." (I did not know until three months later when I was reading my Bible in a Starbucks that is what Jesus said on the cross before giving up His spirit in the book of John) I felt His hand pull away and then it happened. I literally felt every hurt, pain, and addiction leave me at that moment. It was as if Jesus grabbed it and pulled it out of my heart. It was so intense I leaned forward with a great exhale. I didn't have a molecule of oxygen in my lungs it seemed. As I took a breath in to fill my lungs the most incredible thing happened. Something (or someone) entered into me. I felt the deepest part of me get filled with a presence of absolute love, joy, peace, and grace. The only words I have for this feeling was that I finally became alive. At the time I didn't know about the promise Jesus gave about believers receiving the Holy Spirit, but I knew this was the fulfillment of the prayer, "God, come live in my heart."

I felt so energized, alive, and forgiven. Joy was pulsing through my body and I didn't know what to do with myself. I remember thinking that I wanted to run down the streets of my neighborhood and shout and dance all night long. I hopped out of my chair and as my feet hit the floor my legs gave out from underneath me. The presence of God was so strong, my fleshly body couldn't even stand. I laid there on the floor shaking and crying. It was the GREATEST sensation I had ever felt in my life. As I laid there on the floor, I felt an urge rise up inside of me. I had the urge to speak but I didn't know what to say. What on earth could I say in a moment like this? What words could I say to God for giving me such a beautiful freedom? I didn't want to ruin this moment, but the urge became irresistible. I simply opened my mouth and tried to make a sound, but it wasn't just a sound coming out, I began speaking a language I had never heard before in my life. It was as if my spirit took over and my body was along for the ride. I laid there for a long time in the presence of God speaking a language I was clueless of. Eventually, the language stopped, and I just laid on the floor. I didn't want to move.

I could have stayed in that moment forever but then Jesus spoke again. "Son, I want you to do two things. One, start telling people about me and two, honor your wife from this day forward." With tears in my eyes and joy in my heart I agreed saying, "Yes, Jesus, I will." I finally peeled myself off of the floor and stumbled into bed. My wife had remained asleep through the entire thing. I was filled with so much excitement and curiosity. That was the night I KNEW I was saved. I didn't have to hope or wonder if I was going to get into Heaven by the skin of my teeth. I knew Jesus paid the price, that He had forgiven me, and that I was a brand-new person. I wanted to stay up all night praying and talking to God, but I quickly fell into one of the most peaceful sleep I ever had in my life.

The next morning, I heard my wife getting ready to go to work. Normally I sleep in without saying anything to her. I quickly got up and ran to meet her at the front door as she was about to head out. It was definitely a surprise to her to see me up that early and to be practically running after her. "What's wrong? Are you ok?" She asked. I knew if I told her what happened that she most likely wouldn't believe me or it would freak her out so I said, "Babe, something happened to me last night, I'm not going to tell you what it was, I'm going to show you." I gave her a hug and kiss. With a confused and slightly concerned look on her face, she chuckled and went on about her business. I closed the door behind her and stood there looking around the apartment. I could still feel His presence. It felt like I was truly alive for the first time. "Jesus, are you still here in the apartment?" I asked softly outload. "No son." He whispered. "I'm now within you."

After that night, I was a totally different person. October 6th stands as my true day of birth for me. I didn't have a grid for all that happened. I didn't know the technical or theological terms for what had happened. All I knew was that I met Jesus and that I am in deep love with Him and a greater appreciation for my wife and my purpose. All I wanted to do after that night was to get alone with God and talk to Him, read the Bible, and listen to sermons. It felt so pure and so right. I didn't know that there would be a debate or have people doubt what happened. I thought all Christians had the exact same thing, or if they didn't, they would want exactly that.

About six months later after my encounter with Jesus, I found myself volunteering at a church. One of the leaders in the church struck up a conversation with me so we could get to know each other a little more. I remember him asking me, "So Dennis, what do you want to see God do in our church?" I couldn't get my answer out fast enough. I blurted out with great excitement, "I want to see God touch every single person to the point every devil leaves, the Holy Spirit fills their hearts with His love and joy, and that it be so overwhelming we can't even stand on our feet anymore, and we just lie there on the ground speaking in all kinds of different languages!" I thought I gave the perfect answer and that is what all Christians would want. Instead of shared excitement he said, "Whoa, easy bro! You know, not everyone believes in what you believe. Not everyone believes in the baptism of the Holy Spirit and praying in tongues."

I sat there in both shock and excitement. I was shocked that he didn't believe those things happened, but I was also excited because I learned something, "That's what you call it? Baptism of the Holy Spirit and praying in tongues? I'm praying when that happens? That's awesome!" With a more concerned look on the leader's face he asked, "What are you talking about?" To answer his questions I said, "I didn't know there was actually a term for it. All I know is what happened to me." The conversation ended quite quickly after that, but I walked away understanding something. There are many people in the world, Christians included, that still don't know. They don't know of all the things that are available to them being a Christian. They don't know that the Holy Spirit wants to fill them with His power and love. They don't know Jesus still performs miracles, healings, signs, and wonders on the earth today. They don't know that Jesus can set them free of traumatic loss, demonic oppression, and hurts from long ago in their lives. Over time and throughout history, many people have been taught that the outpouring of the Holy Spirit was only for

Pentecost, the healings and miracles ceased with the death of the first Apostles, there is no such thing as speaking in tongues, and that faith is still works based rather than a relationship.

This is what this book is for. This book is to share stories from my life and scriptures from the Bible to show that everything we read in the Bible is still available for today and that Jesus is still Jesus.

TWO

"You missed the best part."

For God did not give us a spirit of fear, but of
power, love, and of sound mind.
2 Timothy 1:7

TWO WEEKS after my encounter with Jesus I was a man on fire. I dedicated every single moment I had to the Lord. I just wanted more of Him. At night, while my wife slept, I would lie in bed and think about Jesus. I could feel His presence in the room. I would try to talk to Him as much as I could before falling asleep.

There were moments though, while in the middle of the night, an odd sense of fear would come over me. The old haunting feeling would attempt to creep back on me. I began thinking of all the things the devil put me through. I'd remember the shadows, the smell, the turning of my stomach, and the misery I had in my heart. I never wanted to go back to that place.

Just as I was reliving all of those memories, I heard a thought enter into my mind, "What if they come back? What if they are really mad and want to get even?" I began being fearful of the very things I got set free from. Millions of thoughts of doubt and my past became the blockbuster movie playing in the theatre of my mind. I came to realize that I was still very afraid of the devil and believed he had the power to ruin my life and hurt me. I was conflicted. I told God that I would trust Him no matter what and I knew that He would protect me, but here I am, lying in bed, full of fear. I knew that I could never beat these things before and that there was only one option I had available, pray.

As I laid face up in my bed, watching the ceiling fan blades turn, I said this prayer:

"Father, I am thankful You set me free from everything. I know You love me and care for me deeply, and now, I do too. But Lord, I need to confess something to You. I am still afraid. I'm afraid the demons are going to return and hurt me or Miranda, and I don't want that. I know if I am being afraid of them, it means I am not trusting You and that will open the door for them to come after me. Jesus, I am literally causing my own self destruction and there is nothing I can do about it. God, TAKE THIS FEAR FROM ME RIGHT NOW."

As soon as I finished the prayer silently in my heart the atmosphere in the small apartment bedroom changed. The sense of dread and fear swallowed the room. My stomach began to turn as I could smell this horrendous smell fill my nostrils. They were back! Still lying in bed, my eyes were on a swivel, scanning the dark room. I remember the dark shadows forming in the room again, but this time, there were way more of them. I counted nine different shadows starting to manifest in the room. They would move in different directions flying around the room and my heart began to pound. I looked over at my wife and she was sound asleep. I knew if I woke her up and told her what was happening, or if she saw what I was seeing, she would never sleep next to me again.

The shadows in the room began to take full form. What were once cloud like objects are now turning into disfigured beasts and began to come close to me. I wanted to jump up and scream but I laid there silently. I remember hearing what sounded like claws ripping up the carpet at the foot of my bed. They drew closer and closer and my adrenaline was in full swing. "Jesus," I prayed to myself, "Please do something, help me." At the split second I was about to jump out of bed and start swinging, kicking, and praying, I felt something touch my rib on the left side of my stomach. You would think that in the middle of a situation like that when something touches you, you would be like a cat thrown onto the ice bath, but that is not what happened. When I felt the touch on my ribs I was instantly filled with peace. The peace was so heavy. My head sunk into the pillow and I fell into a deep sleep.

The next thing I knew, my alarm clock was going off the next morning. My wife had already gotten up and gone to work. I opened my eyes to sunshine beaming through the window and I felt like I slept an entire day. I quickly sat up in bed and looked around. Was it all a dream? Did all of that stuff really happen? I got out of bed and examined the carpet at the foot of the bed expecting to see it torn to shreds...nothing. I walked through the apartment seeing if I could find any evidence of what I saw last night, but I didn't see anything. I got dressed, made breakfast for myself, and sat down on the living room couch. I could feel God's Presence and I felt great. I didn't feel tired and felt peace all around me.

"Jesus, what happened last night?" I asked out loud. I only sat in silence for a few seconds when I heard Him speak with excitement. "Son, I took care of it. You gave me your fear and I handled all of it! I promise, you don't ever have to be afraid of those things coming back. You are mine so don't ever be afraid, son. There is no room for fear in my Kingdom, and if it is not welcome in My kingdom, then it is not welcome in your life either." I sat with tears streaming down my face. It was as if His voice was re-molding my heart and making it more like His. Suddenly, I heard Him laugh and say, "Besides, you missed the best part after you fell asleep." I laughed out loud imagining what all Jesus did last night while I was sleeping. Did a bunch of angels come into the room and have an intense fight or did the devils run away when they saw the angels coming? I don't know, but I do know something happened. Why? Because it changed me.

After that night and since that night I have never been afraid of the demonic. I came to know that the devil has no power whatsoever. He does not have permission to steal, kill, or destroy anything in our lives. The fallen angels also known as demons don't have a right to come and go as they please in my life and my family's life. They may have been stronger than me, but they hold no match to the power and the love of Jesus.

Many nights afterwards, I would wake up from time to time and see a dark figure moving in my room or wherever I may be. I don't ever get scared. I just simply whisper or say the word, "Jesus." Every time I have, the spirit flees immediately. There was one night in particular I saw a few dark figures (demons) attempt to form in my bedroom again. As I saw them, I simply smiled and whispered the word Jesus. As I did, I saw the figures flee and then seven streaks of blue light shot through the room of what looked like lights that were chasing after the figures. I now know that when you call on Heaven to help, they will. Angels are ministering spirits sent to assist those who will inherit salvation. That means angels are sent to help us in our calling and everyday life.

We don't have to live a life oppressed by the darkness and the demonic forces of Satan. We can be free from it all. Because of this encounter, I quickly fell in love with the verse 2 Timothy 1:7 that says, "For God did not give you a spirit of fear, but of power, love, and a sound mind." I've learned that we will either function in one of two ways. We will either function out of fear or we will function out of power, love, and a sound mind. We are designed and empowered by God to live a life of power, and of love, and to have a sound mind. When we live a life functioning in those three things, the devil is absolutely powerless and has no authority or leg to stand on. That is why he attacks us with fear. He knows if he can have a believer trapped in fear, they forfeit living in power, love, and a sound mind. He basically tricks us into putting down our weapons and fighting a fight from a place of disadvantage. Fear is a liar.

Fear of rejection, fear of failure, fear of pain, fear of death, fear of loss, and any other kind of fear doesn't have to be a part of your life. How do you get free from it? The same way I did, you tell Jesus! Jesus is not ashamed of you and is not going to get mad when His children come to Him expressing what is troubling them. Fear makes us feel like we are alienated from God and He never wants to be apart from us. He wants us to be with Him so much, that He sent His Son, Jesus, to pay for all of our sins, so that we could come back to Him. God doesn't want there to be a single barrier between you and Him. No matter what the fear is or what devil you may be facing, if you are willing to stop fighting it on your own and give it to Him, He will remove it in a heartbeat. Jesus is still more powerful than the devil and that will never change.

If you would like help with how to pray for freedom of fear, here is a prayer you can use:

Father, I thank You for the love You have for me. Thank You for all that You have done in, and through, and around my life. Thank You for dying for my sins and overcoming everything that could ever separate me from You. Jesus, there are some fears that I am fighting, and I don't want to fight them anymore. Lord, I am afraid of (list your fears) and I ask You to forgive me for allowing these fears and lies to be a part of my life. I understand that these fears are taking up territory in my heart that You want. Jesus I want You to have all of my heart, so please, take these fears away from me in Jesus name. Come and fill me with Your peace and joy. Teach me how to surrender my thoughts and doubts to You every day of my life. I declare that the devil has no right to my life and that he is defeated by the perfect and complete work of Jesus Christ. I do not have a spirit of fear. I have a spirit of power, and of love, and of a sound mind. I declare, as of right now, fear has lost its grip and I am no longer a slave to fear. I am a child of God and my thoughts are God's thoughts. Thank you Jesus, Amen.

THREE

Signs in the Sky

"You will seek me and find me when you seek me
with all your heart."
Jeremiah 29:13

STILL IN MY early months of being a Christian, I signed up to join a retreat for men through the church I was serving. I really enjoyed events like that. A bunch of good ol' country boys getting together to talk about Jesus and have some fun along the way, I was all about it. I was also excited to just get to meet some other guys that I could develop a friendship with and talk about Jesus. There were about one hundred and fifty men attending the retreat. The whole thing was great, but what I want to share with you is what happened the final morning.

I woke up earlier than usual in my small assigned bunk bed in a cabin with a bunch of dudes snoring and making all kinds of extra noises. A lot of the guys stayed up late playing basketball or just chatting over a game of cards. I quietly got out of my bed and grabbed my shoes, coat, and Bible. I figured this would be a perfect time to go and hang out with Jesus. It was a cold morning and the sun was just beginning to rise. I made my way over to the center section of the retreat where they had a small lake and huge rocks with seating. I sat down on one of the huge rocks that was pointed in the direction of the sunrise that was about to greet the sky. I had some time in the Word and then took a break to watch the sunrise and pray. Bright rays of sun began to illuminate the sky, huge clouds were forming and moving, and colors of purple, orange, and red consumed my eyesight. It was one of those sunrises you could watch the rest of your life and never get tired of.

Then, something caught my attention. In the sky there was a dark cloud that began to take form. It was a big cloud that took up a huge portion of the sky I was looking at. Right before my eyes, the cloud formed into the shape of a beast with huge horns and a spear in its hands. It has the exact same outline as some of the demonic spirits I had seen in the past. "Are you kidding me?" I thought. I was mad and I couldn't believe it. Here I am trying to spend time with Jesus and all I can see now is this cloud that looks like a devil. I couldn't understand why it was there. Did I do something wrong? Why do they keep popping up?

I put my head down, closed my eyes, and started asking God why I was still seeing those types of things. "God, it seems like everywhere I go, they are near. Why do they keep following me and why do I keep seeing them?" After a few minutes I heard the Lord respond. "Son, if you will look for Me as much as you look for them, you will see Me." I was slightly confused about what I heard the Lord saying. I looked back up at the sky and saw that the cloud shaped as a beast had totally transformed. The cloud literally turned into the shape of a hand with a dove flying off of it. I was absolutely shocked. I would close my eyes and look up again thinking there was something wrong with my sight. It never changed until the cloud floated away and out of sight. I sat there on the rock puzzled at what just happened and wondered if I was going crazy.

The time came for breakfast and I was still lost in thought. I sat at a round table with five other men I was still getting to know. I remained quiet throughout the breakfast as the other men talked. I was trying to put all the puzzle pieces together in my head of what I saw and what God said.

I started doubting what I saw and thought it was all just my imagination until the man across the table from me asked, "The sky looked a little different this morning didn't it?" My eyes shot up towards him. He kept his gaze on his plate as he used his fork to break up his eggs.

"What did you say?" I asked to confirm if I really heard him ask that. The man took a sip of coffee and stared at me, "I said, the sky looked a little different this morning, didn't it?"

I was stunned by the question and quickly asked, "Did you see it?" "No" the man immediately replied, "but you did, didn't you?" I felt my heart jump with excitement and awe. "How did you know to ask me that?" At this time everyone at the table is listening to our conversation. "I just felt like God told me you saw something in the sky this morning and He wanted me to tell you that you really saw it."

At that point I had tears in my eyes and didn't even know what to say. God was so good to me to show me the amazing sign in the clouds, tell me what it meant, and then give me a friend to confirm what I saw. I then shared the story with the other men at the table. Of course, to most of them it was a far-fetched story, but to the man sitting across from me, he understood.

Here is what I learned from that encounter and what God was teaching me. He was teaching me to look for Him in my life. After all of the oppression and bullying I took from the devil, I found myself in a constant state of looking for where the next attack was going to come from. I had trained myself to look for the kingdom of darkness rather than the kingdom of Heaven. The Lord revealed to me that if we are able to hear or see the demonic, we have access and permission to see the angelic and the things of the Kingdom of Heaven. It is not a one-sided thing. We have full access to the Kingdom of Heaven for those who are in Christ Jesus. I've heard people say, "There is a devil under every rock." I don't know if that statement is true or not but what I do know is that demons were once a third of the angels in Heaven until they rebelled against God. So, that means for every devil there are two angels.

The angels outnumber them two to one. What good does it do to try to find the devil everywhere we go? We don't need to look for them, we need to look for Him. If you look for devils, you will find them. If you look for Heaven, you will encounter it. I decided that morning to quit looking for the devil everywhere I went and started looking for what Heaven was doing. Since that time, I've had more encounters with Heaven that I ever did have with the demonic.

Another important lesson I learned from this was how to view people. Jesus is not sin conscious in Heaven. He is not pacing back and forth in the throne room of Heaven wondering what He is going to do about our sins. He's already taken care of all that.

That means, Jesus is not looking at what is wrong with us. He looks at what is right with us and what is needed. He sees our potential and who He calls us to be. With that, He has a strategy on how we can become the person He has designed us to be. Since that is how he views people, that is the way we need to view them also. This lesson taught me to look for Heaven in people, meaning, look at what is good in them. Look at their strengths and what Jesus is doing. Call out their strengths instead of searching for faults and weaknesses. If we are not careful, we can become judgmental and hypocritical by looking for a person's faults and failures rather than looking for what Heaven is doing or is wanting to do in their life.

The final thing I learned from this encounter is that Jesus still performs signs and wonders. The Bible says that signs and wonders will follow those who believe. In the book of Acts, Jesus said there would be wonders above in the Heavens and signs in the earth below. These things did not stop happening. There are some people who believe that signs and wonders are not for today because we now have the Bible. They will say, "Signs and wonders are no longer necessary because we have the Bible." But I just don't see God giving us a book so He could become distant and quiet. He gave us His Word so we could learn more about who He is and know of all the authority, power, and permission we have in Him. If we believe in Jesus with all our heart and want to live a life of loving Him well, signs and wonders will follow us everywhere we go. Jesus still wants to interact with His creation every day and all the time. Jesus is still Jesus.

FOUR

Love them all

"Be completely humble and gentle; be patient,
bearing with one another in love."
Ephesians 4:2

I REALIZE that the last chapter might have been a little heavy for
some people. I thought about putting those stories towards the
end of the book to help some readers warm up to what I'm talking
about, but these are the events that happened to me in order. I
didn't get much of a chance to be "ready" for what was to come in
my life. I think that is an amazing thing to learn and know. Most
things God wants to do in your life, you will not be ready for. He
does that to show us that it is Him doing the things that are
happening and it is outside of our own power, will, and control. I
also wanted to show that a "baby" Christian like myself had power
in Jesus to overcome any demonic strategy or oppression that was
thrown at me. Overcoming the attacks of the devil has nothing to
do with skill or gifting, but everything to do with loving Jesus well.

Satan is known in the Bible to be a deceiver. He knows the truth but is incapable of expressing it. Every word from his mouth is a lie. He doesn't have an ounce of compassion and has no hope whatsoever. The Bible is very clear that his agenda is to steal, kill, and destroy. Again, God's Word says he is like a roaring lion, who seeks to devour. So, with that understanding, what benefit is it to focus on him? If every word or spiritual influence that comes from him is false, misleading, and destructive, why pay it any attention? If we do, we become consumed with what he wants. He wants us to believe every challenge in life is betrayal from God, every sickness is going to cause our death, we are not good enough, strong enough, and when we encounter oppressed people we need to address every devil in their life. These strategies pull our hearts from rest to distress, from abundance to lack, to fighting from victory to towards it. Focusing on the devil is like being in a boxing match and doing what your opponent's coach tells you.

Jesus made the Gospel simple enough for children to understand. The two greatest commandments are "Love the Lord your God with all your heart, soul, and strength. And the second is like the first, love your neighbor as yourself." When we love Jesus well, we come into a greater understanding of who He is and who we are. Through that, we have our identity intact. We are no longer wavering to the opinions of other people. The only way to be free from other people is to be free from ourselves. If we spend our entire life battling who we are, we will always be in opposition with ourselves. If we are complicated in our own eyes, we have ushered in the spirit of chaos to come and make life miserable and confusing. But, when our hearts become Jesus' throne, when we hear His voice tell us who we are, and are set free from all other voices, lies, and opinions, we are truly free to love others as we love ourselves. We are no longer looking at what is wrong with other people because we are no longer looking at what is wrong with ourselves. What I mean is, we are not focused on the 'devils' a person has and we are able to see them from the perspective of how God sees them. When we can see people in that perspective, we can be used to do serious damage to the enemy, without even acknowledging him. Does that mean I never cast out devils? Of course I'll cast out devils, but my focus is not them, my focus is the beautiful person they are oppressing.

When I sit down to meet with people and talk to them about spiritual warfare or overcoming the attacks of the enemy, I start out by telling them, "You know, the sheep never has to be afraid of the wolves, because their best friend is the lion." What I mean by this is, in the world, we are like sheep. We need a shepherd to guide us and nurture us. Also, in the world, are wolves. The wolves are those that seek to do harm to the body of Christ or spiritual forces that are on a quest to steal, kill, and destroy. The wolves want to hunt down the sheep and destroy them, but the good news is we have a Lion for a best friend. Of course, I am referring to the one that is called the Lion of Judah, Jesus. As long as we stay close to Him, the wolves have to tread carefully. However, the moment a sheep ventures away from the protection of the lion, the wolves will start hunting again. It is imperative to stay close to the Lion in our lives, to cling close to the hem of Jesus' robe.

Also, when I am explaining this concept, I tell people, "Do you know what the beautiful thing is about a sheep being best friends with a lion? We are around the lion so much; we begin to act like him. We see how He handles situations and carries Himself. We see His courage, passion, and intensity. The more we are around Him, the more we become like Him. It is the exact same with Jesus. The more we are around Him; we see what He is like. We understand the way He speaks, the joy that He has, the certainty of who He is, and it builds us up and transforms us to be more like Him.

I would also like to add this point, since we can hang out with the "Lion" and learn how to be like Him, we can end up doing the same thing with "wolves". When we let people into our lives that are not kingdom minded and influence us to live a life that is not holy, we will then begin to act like them. Relationships that fuel our pride or mask our insecurities are not real relationships. Many people end up in horrible and toxic relationships simply because they don't know who Jesus says they are and it leads them to insecurity. The insecurity breeds a fear of loneliness, and that lures them into any type of relationship for the sake of not being alone. Pride will keep us from confronting sins or past hurts. Often, what we do is associate with people who have the same sin or past hurts and that gives us a false sense of comfort. We think, "Well, if my friends aren't addressing the problem, why should I?" I think it is very important for every believer to constantly pray, "God, put the right people in my life, and keep the wrong ones away."

The sheep have to make a choice; stay with the lion and learn how to become like one or, venture away and be consumed by the wolves. Jesus is still our protector and even when we venture away from Him, He is always willing to welcome us back into His love, grace, and protection when we turn around.

So, with that being said, after having the experiences of freedom, I had a burning desire to see everyone else in the world encounter the same thing. I wanted everyone to see Jesus for who He really is and for everyone to be free from what is destroying them on the inside. The Bible talks about how our warfare is not against flesh and blood, but against the rulers, authorities, principalities, and dark spiritual forces. I realized that if I ever encounter a person who is being difficult or harsh, my problem is not them, but with the spirit that is affecting them. Before Jesus, if someone was rude to me or belittled me, I instantly wanted to retaliate and see justice. I wanted them to be taught a lesson. After Jesus, I learned the people who are hurtful are hurting within. They are drowning in some type of trauma or experience from their past that introduced some type of oppression in their life. This revelation gave me compassion for those who are like that. I could finally see through the attitude and harshness and see someone who was hurt and lost. It's a good thing I learned that before my anniversary vacation to Mexico.

My wife and I decided to go to Mexico on our anniversary. We made our way to the airport and were waiting at the gate for boarding. As we waited, a group of six friends arrived at the gate. They were excited and quite vocal of all the partying they had planned on doing while in Mexico. One of the guys in the group was in a mode I like to call "peacock mode." He was a broad shouldered guy and he had his chest puffed out and flexed his arms as he walked. Underneath his unbuttoned Hawaiian was a gray shirt that said, "'Blank' YOU I'M ON VACA!" Of course, the blank wasn't blank. He paced around the gate staring at people and sizing everyone up. He would cut up with his friends, being very loud with explicit language, and then he started staring at me. I couldn't help but stare back. We had this unusual little standoff of staring at each other and he would make a motion with his arms as if saying, "What?"

He appeared to be an angry tough guy, but on the inside, I knew he was broken and hurt and that I was going to have the opportunity to talk to him. I leaned towards my wife, "Babe, see the guy with the hat and the shirt with curse words on it?" She looked over at him and said, "Yeah, what about him?" "I guarantee you, before this trip is over, I'm going to get to have a heart to heart talk with him." My wife laughed. "I bet I'll even give him a hug." She laughed even more but also advised me to quit making eye contact with him.

The time finally came for us to board the plane. My wife and I were sitting in the back. We got settled into our seats and up ahead I saw my new buddy getting on the plane. He did his normal tough guy stare down to everyone around him and then our eyes locked. He gave me a glare and I responded with the biggest smile I could give along with a child-like wave. It was comical. It instantly confused him to why I would be responding to him in this manner and he got in his seat quickly. We finally landed in Mexico and there were tourists everywhere going in every direction to take a bus or shuttle to get to their resort. There are hundreds of resorts in Mexico, but guess who was staying at the same resort as me? Yep, Hawaiian shirt tough guy!

We saw the crew of friends again at check in, "Babe, it's them! They are at the same resort as us! Isn't that cool? God is totally going to do something?" I said to my wife. My wife was still getting used to the new me at this time. I had been changed just a few years before and I wasn't as outgoing or bold before. She just smiled, laughed, and then carried on about her business. This was uncharted territory for the both of us. I wasn't the type of guy to share Jesus with random strangers and she wasn't quite used to the boldness that was coming out of me.

As our vacation proceeded, we ended up having many encounters with the group of friends and all of them were the same. The tough guy would yell at me, curse at me, or even throw something at me. One time he threw a football at my face. I quickly dodged it and stared back at him. He yelled and cursed at me again. I responded, "Bro, if you keep that up, I'm going to come over there and give you a hug!" I think he and I were both shocked that I said that. "What?" He yelled across from the pool with everyone around watching and listening. "I said, I'm going to come over there and give you a hug! It's obvious that is what you need. You just need a hug bro." Everyone laughed except him.

This happened on repeat the next two days. He would do something, and I would just put my arms up inviting him for a hug. He absolutely hated it. It got so bad that many other people in the resort noticed the back and forth interactions we were having. I didn't care how rude he was. I wanted him to be free.

It was the last full day for Miranda and me at the resort. We had an amazing time together and enjoyed every moment together. I didn't let the tough guy ruin my vacation. My wife and I were sitting at the pool enjoying the view just before lunch. I looked over to my right and saw a tough guy stumbling out of his room and into the pool area. You could tell he was extremely hung over. He then put on a mask that Hispanic wrestlers wear to cover up his face. I knew something wasn't right. He looked discouraged and slightly embarrassed for some reason. His head was held low. No longer was he in peacock mode. He looked over at me and I offered the same friendly wave I gave before. He stared for a moment and then finally picked up one hand and waved reluctantly and then he jumped into the pool and started swimming slowly over to me. I looked over at my wife who saw the tough guy swimming to us, "Guess what babe?" I said with a loud whisper, "It's about to happen!"

The tough guy swam over and sat up right next to me on the ledge of the pool. "Yo!" he said. "What's up with the mask man? You good?" I asked him as he still had his head low. "I'm kind of embarrassed, man." "What for?" I asked. He then continued to tell me about the day he had before. He ended up leaving the resort and went partying. He ended up losing all of his money and his shoes. After that, he came back to the hotel and made quite the embarrassing scene in the restaurant. Apparently, it was so bad, he had to be escorted to his room and he was facing a fine for damages he made in the restaurant. He was lucky they didn't kick him out.

"So, you had a rough night?" I asked him. "Take your mask off bro. One bad night doesn't define you and besides, everyone here knows it's you under that mask." We both chuckled and he pulled the mask off. "That's not all of it though." He explained. "It seems like I'm always messing up." There it was, the perfect opportunity! We continued talking. He did most of the talking and I did most of the listening. It was a very bizarre turn. This tough guy was cursing at me the day before and now he was sharing his heart about hurts and pains from the past. What did I do for this to happen? I kept showing love. I was real with him but didn't speak as though I was better than him, or that I had life all figured out. I related with him in his struggles and then began encouraging him.

He knew his mistakes; I didn't need to remind him. What he needed to hear was how God sees him and how he should see himself. I told him my story in a receivable manner and told him who Jesus was. I didn't force it on him but made it clear that Jesus was the way out of the mess he shared with me. He then swam away, not before I was able to pray with him and give him a hug!

Jesus is always humble, kind, and gentle with us. There are days we completely mess things up. But in those days, His love never changes for us. He is always so kind and caring to allow us to come back to Him so he can comfort us and speak life into us. The Church has to be the same way. We have to quit viewing people as the problem. No matter who the person is or what they have done, they are a beautiful and unique creation with a destiny and call on their life. The only opposition we face is the one that is hurting them as well. They are victims and slaves to the oppressions on their life. Treating them harshly or with violence is not going to help them or you. We have to be like Jesus. We have to be kind and caring even if they are not kind and caring to us.

During the entire situation I felt a grace be poured out over me. It was like I could constantly see the bigger picture of the situation. I wasn't a biblical scholar or a popular preacher. I was just a son trying to do what Jesus would have done. I was just a sheep trying to copy the lion. Because I learned that some of the wolves we think we have in our lives are not wolves, they are just hurt sheep. Jesus still wants to use everyone. He wants to fill us with his love, joy, and peace. He wants His power coursing through our bodies, and to have an eternal relationship with him forever. To be used by God, it is not about our abilities, it is about our availability. If you want to see God move in, through, and around your life, all you have to do is be available.

FIVE

Where did he go?

"Do not forget to show hospitality to strangers,
for by so doing some people have shown
hospitality to angels without knowing it."
Hebrews 13:2

LET'S fast forward the story a little bit, shall we? It is now 2014. I
had been following the Lord for about three years. I was now
working full time at my local church and was attending a seminary that our pastor was leading. I was constantly having visions
during the day and dreams at night of seeing huge crowds of
people getting saved. That year was when I learned about Gospel
Crusades. Gospel Crusades are when Evangelists partner with the
local Church in an area and host a multi-day outdoor event where
the Evangelist preaches the Gospel. Many people get saved at
these types of events along with healings, miracles, deliverances,
and all the new believers get connected to the local Church. I
immediately fell in love with the idea of Gospel Crusades. I would

research crusades for hours. I loved watching videos on YouTube and hearing all the testimonies of people being healed and delivered. I would shake and cry every time I watched one of those videos.

Also, during that time, I was having trouble believing that God wanted to use me to heal people in Jesus name. I read about healings and miracles in the Bible, I believed they still happened, I just didn't think God could use me to do it. I had prayed for people to be healed but never really saw anything happen. This thought weighed on me for over a year. I greatly desired to see healings and miracles. I would ask God every day for it. I eventually went to my pastor to talk to him about the desire to do crusades and to see people healed. He suggested that I should go to a crusade and watch the evangelist and see how they do things and try to have the team there pray for me to receive the gift. I loved the idea. I did some research and saw that a powerful evangelist I respected was going to be in Houston doing a crusade. I booked a hotel and took off to Houston.

When I got to Houston, I had an expectation of what God was going to do. How many of you know God will work in ways you least expect it? My greatest encounter in Houston didn't happen during the crusade, it happened while I was waiting in line to get in.

I arrived at the crusade a few hours before it started. The stadium was huge, and people were already in line to get in. I found the back of the line and settled in. Where I stood was in a very open spot. I could see the entrance to the stadium in front of me. To my right were some trees and benches where some older people were sitting. To my left was the street with buses, parking lots, and police coordinating traffic. While I waited in line, I noticed a man up at the front of the line. He appeared to be homeless. His clothes were torn and rugged, he was carrying a small bag over his shoulder, and looked unshaven.

The man was going down the line trying to talk to people. He was far away from me so I couldn't tell at first what he was saying to the people in line. I did notice though that no one was giving him a response or their time. Even though many people were ignoring him, he continued to go down the line. I was very curious and drawn to him. It was weird, I literally couldn't stop watching this guy. Finally, he had worked his way down in front of me where he was close enough, I could hear what he was saying to people. I realized he was asking people a question. He would point directly at the person he was talking to and with a raspy voice ask, "Why do you love Jesus?" He would simply ask the question and wait for the person to respond. He would ask the same question and still got the same responses. Sometimes people would give him a very quick answer or just simply ignore him.

I couldn't wait for him to get to me. I wanted to tell him about my past and about what happened in 2011. He finally made his way to me. He did the exact same thing to me as he did the others. He pointed at my chest and asked, "Why do you love Jesus?" To spare you the story again, let's just say I crammed all of chapter one in this book into thirty seconds in conversation with him.

As I finished telling the man that I had been totally changed by God and that I want to live the rest of my life for him, I noticed how deeply he was staring at me. It was as if he was looking right through me, but he didn't say anything. To try to break up the awkward silence I asked him, "What about you? Do you love Jesus?" The man smiled at me and continued on down the line.

I turned around to watch him be dismissed by the rest of the people. Sadly, the group of people behind me made a few comments about the man and laughed. The gate had still not opened for us to enter the crusade, so I just kept watching the man go down the line talking to people. After he went all the way to the end of the block, he made his way over to the trees and park benches that were on my right-hand side. He stood between two trees watching people walk by. He then set his gaze on an older couple sitting down at the benches. He slowly made his approach to them but got dismissed by them even before he could say anything. He stepped away from them and shrugged his shoulders with a deep exhale. There was something about the guy and I wanted to talk to him again.

I watched him until he finally looked in my direction. When I knew he could see me I waved my arms at him and motioned for him to come back towards me. He stared for just a moment and then began making his way to me. The people behind me started making remarks, "Oh great, he's coming back." I turned and politely smiled and by that time my new friend had made it back over to me. As he approached, he stood very close to me, honestly, it was almost uncomfortable. I started the conversation,

"Hey bro, what is your name?" "Rikki." He replied. I reached out my hand to offer a handshake, "It's nice to meet you Rikki. So, what is your story? Do you know Jesus?"

All of a sudden Rikki started putting me through a Bible quiz. He began quoting different Bible verses and asked me who said it or wrote it. "I am the way, the truth, and the life. Who said that?" Rikki asked. "Jesus said that." I replied. He kept asking me more and more and they were getting harder. The final one he asked, "Who said, by His stripes we are healed?" I answered him, "Isaiah said that about Jesus. Jesus was lashed thirty-nine times on his back, and it was to pay for our healing." Keep in mind I was struggling in my own heart that God would even want to use me to heal. Rikki smiled and was pleased with my answer and then he said, "You know, there is only one thing that is holding me back in this life." Before he could say anything else or before I could even think, I suddenly smelled alcohol very strongly.

Rikki had been standing literally just over one foot from me, talking, and asking me questions, and I didn't smell the alcohol until he said something was holding him back. I found that very unusual. I felt bad for Rikki. He had been going up to everyone wanting to talk about Jesus and now he is telling me about how alcohol is holding him back. Well, we've gone all this way. No sense in stopping now,I thought to myself.

"Are you talking about alcohol?" I finally asked him. He had a slight grin on his face and shook his head in agreement. "Well, that thing can die." I said to him. I wanted to see this man get set free. I wanted to see him get set free more than being worried of looking dumb or unsuccessful in prayer.

The people again behind me murmured in their discomfort of the situation and Rikki heard them, "Don't worry about them buddy. Will you let me pray for you and ask Jesus to take away the alcohol right now?" With a big smile on his face he said, "Yes, I would like that very much." As I was about to pray the Lord told me to ask for his name again. I didn't want to because normally I am bad with names and this time I had remembered. I felt the urgency of the Lord and I knew that He really wanted me to ask and that it was important. So, I put my hand on the man's shoulder and asked, "Hey, before I pray, remind me of your name again." He threw me off with his reply. "My real name is Raphael." I went along with it and said, "Ok Raphael, I am going to pray for you and let Jesus do what He wants to do in your life." I put my hand on Rikki Raphael's chest and started praying out loud.

As I was praying, I glanced up at him and noticed he was doing the stare again. The focus and intensity in his eyes reminded me of a fire but there was also a calming peace about him. I finished praying for him and the smell of alcohol disappeared. I invited him to come and sit with me in the crusade. He declined and said, "No, I have everything I need now." I leaned in and gave him a hug. As he turned to walk away, I turned to the people behind me and asked, "Wasn't that awesome?" I was hoping my enthusiasm for the moment would cause them to reconsider how they thought of people.

I turned back around, and Raphael was gone!

I couldn't find him anywhere. I literally turned away from him for two seconds and he was nowhere to be found. I could see far in every direction. It would take at least thirty seconds for him to get out of my range of sight. I even asked the people in line to help me look for him. None of us were successful in locating him. He simply vanished.

After about twenty more minutes of standing in line and looking for my friend, the gates opened, and we went in for the crusade. I enjoyed every moment of the event and got to see God do amazing miracles through the evangelist, but I couldn't shake the thought of Raphael. Something in my heart told me something very special happened in that time of waiting in line. The next day I packed my bags and headed back home. I later on met up with a mentor of mine and started to tell him the story. I made it halfway through when my mentor interrupted me saying, "You know that was not a man, right?" I hadn't even told him about the disappearing trick, the way he stared, or about his name. "Dennis, that was an angel. I guarantee you the Lord sent him there to see who would be willing to do what you did for him." It all made sense to me, but I also couldn't help but ask, "Why me?"

My mentor asked, "What did he say his name was?" I replied, "Well, at first he said his name was Rikki but after I offered to pray for him, he told me his real name was Raphael." My mentors' eyes lit up and motioned me to follow him to his office. He sat at his computer and began typing. "What's up man? What do you think it means?" I asked curiously. He hit the enter button hard with a single finger and then showed me what was on his screen. The website he pulled up had information about angels that are in Heaven, and one of those angel's names is Raphael. My mouth dropped open. Even more, my mentor showed me that Raphael is in charge of healing. Is this really happening to me? Did I really just encounter an angel?

I was terrified to tell anyone about this encounter for quite some time. I probably would have written the situation off as an odd coincidence but there was a tremendous change in my life. I noticed after that night; people were getting miraculously healed when I would pray for them. I will share some of those stories later on in the book along with teaching and encouragement on how to minister healing. The reason why I share this story is to point out that Heaven still wants to move here on earth. We are not called to walk this life alone. Angels are like the UPS or FedEx of heaven. God sends angels to assist us in our calling. We don't need to worship the angels, but we do need to be aware that Heaven is very active and that we can have a partnership with them.

All throughout the Bible we read about people encountering the angelic. From Genesis to Revelation the Bible is covered in these encounters. Jesus is still on the throne and He sends His angels to partner with us and help us. Angels are not just commissioned to "super Christians." They are sent to help all of us. You may be asking; how do I encounter something like that? What do I need to do? Here is what I recommend. Make sure you are loving God and other people well and the rest will fall into place. What I also learned was that the nonstop conflict in my heart about healing was actually from God. He was working on my heart and preparing me to receive that impartation and/or gift of healing. Has there been something you have been wrestling with for months or years that you want to see God do through your life, but have trouble believing God could use you to do it? You are in good company. Whether it is healing, deliverance, being prophetic, or any other type of gift, if it has been heavy on your heart for a long time, it is an indicator that God is getting you ready to inherit and receive the impartation of the gift. Just keep pursuing the Lord and know that he is excited about this season of your life and in the right time, you will receive the breakthrough and the provision.

SIX

Her Eyes Opened
_____

*"Go into all the world and preach the gospel to
all creation. Whoever believes and is
baptized will be saved, but whoever does not
believe will be condemned. And these signs
will accompany those who believe: In my
name they will drive out demons; they will
speak in new tongues; they will pick up
snakes with their hands; and when they
drink deadly poison, it will not hurt them at
all; they will place their hands on sick people
and they will get well."*
Mark 16:15-18

SEEING God do healings and miracles through me was a process.
For me, there was a lot of wrestling with myself. After my
encounter in Houston I knew things were different, but I didn't
know just how different. My heart ached to see people get healed.

I didn't want to see people get healed so I could appear to be great or to have someone pat me on the back and say, "Wow, you are a powerful Christian." I wanted to see it because the Bible is full of stories of people being totally transformed by the healing touch of Jesus and I wasn't seeing it anywhere around me or my community. Also, there was a divine discontentment in my heart. Every Sunday I would see people coming into church with sickness, pain, and injuries, and they would leave with them. In stores, I would see people in wheelchairs, limping, or other physical ailments. No matter where I went in that time all I could see was the need for healing. Not just so bodies could be fixed, but also for people to see that God is not distant and deaf. He is near and wants us to tangibly experience His presence, love, and power.

I would spend hours on YouTube watching testimony videos of people getting miraculously healed. I couldn't help but shake and cry as I watched. I begged God, "Lord, please use me like that. What do I need to do to be used in that way?" Many times, I thought I wasn't special enough to be able to pray for the sick or that the small struggles I was facing disqualified me. I was caught in this inner conflict.

I knew God could do it, I knew there was a need, I desired it greatly, but I just didn't think I was the right kind of vessel. Many times, in my life I struggled with insecurity. I've had to fight off the feeling of not being good enough, strong enough, or smart enough. I realized that this cycle I was in wasn't helpful. It was similar to the feeling I had about needing to be set free from the attacks of the devil when I first got saved. I knew it was a situation outside of my control and the only way to have breakthrough was to surrender it to Jesus.

So, that's what I did.

Jesus, I know you can heal. I know you have the power to heal people and set people free. I want you to use me to bring healing to your people. I'm going to be honest with you, I don't feel like I'm good enough or that you don't want to use me. Your word says we will receive power when the Holy Spirit comes upon us. So, God, in faith, I am asking you to put me in a situation where I can have the faith to pray for the sick and for them to be healed.

I had reached a tipping point. My desire had become greater than my doubt. I reached a point in my heart where I didn't care if I embarrassed myself praying for people and they didn't get healed. I realized it wasn't up to me. I don't take the credit when someone gets healed and I don't take the guilt if they don't. I was all in. God had been preparing my heart the entire time and something big was just around the corner.

I got a text from a fellow pastor I worked with. I had expressed to him how much I wanted to see healing and that I was concerned that we were not operating in that. He was always willing to help me and coach me through the processes of ministry. He was actually the pastor who suggested and sent me to Houston to watch the crusade. The text he sent me was about a prayer meeting that was going to happen in just a few moments in our conference room, and he asked me to join them. I quickly finished up what I was doing and made my way to the meeting room. As I walked in there was the pastor and three other staff members.

As we sat down, the pastor told us, "Hey. Thanks for coming in short notice. There is a couple on their way right now to be prayed for. The wife of the couple has been blind for most of her life and she is wanting us to pray for her,and the husband is bringing her now."

I couldn't believe it. I was excited and terrified at the same time. We didn't have to wait long, and the couple entered the meeting room. They were an older couple that spent most of their life living up north. They were a sweet couple that loved to lightly pick at each other and tease with jokes. The husband was leading his wife by the arm into the room. We had a lot of circle tables with chairs set up. As he led her in, she would often bump into a chair or table, and she would quickly throw her hand down to see what she hit to maneuver around it. Once she got seated, we all introduced ourselves and asked if she could share what was going on and how we could help her. She shared her story about her life and her condition. As she spoke, I could see what looked like scales over her eyes. All she could see were blurs. If a person was standing in front of her all she would see is a fuzzy outline. She then shared with us that the doctors are wanting to do injections on her eyes. She had the same type of procedure done before and it caused a tremendous amount of pain, on top of all that, it was unsuccessful.

As she shared her situation, she became emotional. "Could you all please pray for me? Pray for God to fix my eyes, so I don't have to have injections in them." As she said that my feet and hands started shaking. I couldn't control it. There was a sense of compassion swelling up in my heart like never before. It was odd, I knew something was about to happen, but I was still nervous and, to be honest, scared. As I looked around the room, I noticed the pastor and the other staff workers were staring at me. The pastor then asked, "Alright, who wants to pray for her?"

Without even giving myself time to think, I quickly stood up and said, "Me... I'll do it." It felt like slow motion walking over to her. I took her by the hand and began to encourage her and explain how I was going to pray for her. I asked for permission to put my hand over her eyes while I prayed. She graciously allowed me to. It was like time stood still. It wasn't like this for every healing moment I've seen, this one was very different. I'm guessing since it was my first time to really step out and I had so many different emotions going through my mind is why it felt the way it did. I'm going to be honest with you. When I put my hand over her eyes, I didn't have that "I know she is going to be healed" feeling. I just had compassion and love for her. I didn't see her as an older lady with bad eyes. I saw her as a little girl that was a child of God.

As I prayed, I thanked God for her life. I thanked Him for being so amazing, and then I started commanding her eyes to be healed. I wasn't asking them to heal.... I told them to be healed. I commanded blindness to leave and said to her eyes, "You will open in Jesus name." I finished praying and pulled my hands away. "Sweetheart, I want you to try and look around and let me know if you can see anything." She wiped tears from her eyes and started to test her vision. "To be honest, it actually is a little better." My heart lit up. I was excited there was progress, but I wasn't going to stop there.

I asked if I could pray for her again and did so. As I pulled my hands away, I asked her to do the same thing as earlier. I could tell she was squinting really hard and wasn't wanting to answer. "You don't have to be nice to me. If your vision didn't improve, let me know." She exhaled and said, "Sorry sweetie. No change that time." I paused and thought for just a moment. "This can't be it," I thought to myself. Jesus didn't just half heal in the Bible and he didn't just half die on the cross. This can't end this way.

"Ok sweetheart, one more time! Let's do this." The third time I placed my hand over her eyes I felt intense heat coming through my hands. I could feel the presence of the Lord in the room. I finished my prayer and I pulled my hand away, "How about now?" I asked as she immediately started looking around the room. Her eyes were wide open, more than before. Her mouth dropped open as if she were marveling at something. She then looked directly at me, which was something she couldn't do earlier, and she said, "You have beautiful brown eyes."

Immediately tears of joy ran down my face along with everyone else in the room. The husband reached over and kissed his sweet wife on both eyes. After a moment of crying we began to test her vision. She went from only seeing blurry objects to knowing the details of people's faces. She even made a joke to her husband, "I thought you would be better looking than this." We all started laughing and then we all prayed together praising God for what He just did. As she and her husband left the room, she left without any assistance from her husband, and never did bump into a single chair or table. That was my first major healing.

After that day, healings became very frequent. I could tell you stories about the deaf and mute teenager from Kenya who got radically healed in an instant. The Pastor in India who had a paralyzed arm for more than ten years suddenly gets touched by Jesus and regained full mobility and strength in his arm, or the woman who couldn't feel her legs for four years got out of her wheelchair and walked, the tumor the size of a lemon in a man's brain that disappeared overnight after we prayed, the little baby with stage three cancer who is now cancer free, about the villager who had one leg shorter than the other that grew out to the same length as the other, all the way to the headaches that were healed, the colds and sore throats that vanished, and the ear infections that healed, all of them were healed by Jesus, along with thousands more.

There is a theology in the world today that teaches Jesus doesn't heal anymore, but I am here to tell you, that is a false doctrine. In my life, I always choose the doctrine that makes Jesus more and me less. I choose to believe in a Gospel that is full and complete. I choose to believe that Jesus cares about every aspect of our lives. No matter how great or how small, He cares about it all, and he wants to use His children to bring hope and healing to the world. Jesus said, "If you believe in me, you will do the works I have been doing, and they will do greater things than these." The Bible also says there is not enough paper and storage to hold all the testimonies of what Jesus did on the earth. He healed the sick, cast out devils, cleansed the lepers, and raised the dead. We are called to do the same thing. It has nothing to do with your talents or your failures, it has everything to do with who He is and who He calls us to be. It is His will for people to be healed through prayer. He wants us to be in partnership with Him in seeing these things through. The book of Mark says Jesus worked with them and confirmed his word that accompanied it. Jesus still heals and he wants to heal you and also wants to use you to heal others. Jesus is still Jesus. When praying for people, it's not about how you feel and it's not about what you do see or don't see. It all comes down to God's word. The final authority in our life needs to be what is said in His word. We hold fast onto His promises and we don't allow sight or feeling to ever hinder that.

There are some practical things you can do when praying for the sick and injured. First of all, it is important to involve them. Allow them to tell you their story and all the events that have led to this moment (time permitting). Give them the opportunity to share as much as they want or as little as they want. A lot of times I like to ask the person what they want out of the prayer. A few years ago, I had a family member who fell and broke her back. When she fell, she was immediately rushed to the hospital. The doctors did many scans and tests on her back and revealed a fracture in her lower spine. She was in intense pain and was put in a back brace to stabilize her spine. After a lot of discussion and since she was a young teenager, they decided to put her on bed rest to see if her body would self-heal the fracture. She went home and spent a few weeks in bed. As time progressed the self-healing plan did not look promising. They told her most likely she would need to have a spinal fusion surgery to fix her back. When I received word of her circumstance, I knew the situation wasn't right. I felt faith starting to stir in my heart that God wanted to heal her. My wife reached out to the family and asked if we could come over to pray. The next day we got in our car and drove over to their house.

As my wife and I walked into her room you could tell that she was tired and frustrated with being in bed for so long and being strapped into an uncomfortable back brace. I pulled up a chair next to her and asked her to tell me about the injury and the events that led up to it. I've learned a lot of times; people think the only reason you have the faith to pray for them is because you don't know the whole story. I've had some individuals say, "Well, if you knew how much I've been through, all the pain I've endured, and what all the doctors said, you might not be as confident praying for me." So, I make sure they tell me as much as they feel comfortable. I want them to tell me what the doctors said can and can't happen. I want them to know that I know exactly what they have been through, and yet, I still believe Jesus can and will heal them.

After she shared her story, I began to share my own stories with her. I told her testimonies of people getting healed that were in worse shape. As I shared those stories with her, I taught her what the Bible said about healing and how Jesus still does those things to this very day. I'm telling her these things to do two things. One, to build up her faith, and two, to let her know that what I'm telling her is biblical and not just some crazy idea in my head. Once I share those things with a person, I begin to tell them how much God loves them. Sadly, many people feel like they are not good enough to be healed or that they are not special enough. I know what that is like, so, I make sure to reinforce that God loves them and still cares for them today, and that He is not punishing them.

Finally, after stories, testimonies, and encouragement is given, I ask them the questions. "Ok, I'm about to pray for you. What do you want to happen?" For the young girl specifically, the question was. "What do you want God to do right here, right now? We can pray one of two ways. We can pray that God slowly heals your back so you don't have to have surgery, or we can pray God miraculously and completely heals your back right now and you get out of bed and go on with your life. Which one do you want?" Of course, for me, I want to pray the second, but I think it is important to give people ownership of what they want to happen. I told her, "Sweetheart, I'm good with either prayer, but I want to be in agreement with you and what you want." She laid there thinking for a moment and then responded, "Let's pray that I don't need surgery."

"Great! So, you are going with option 1?" I asked to verify. She nodded her head in agreement. I know as some people read this; they may be disappointed. "What a lack of faith." You might think. But why? Why is it a lack of faith that she chose the healing rather than the instantaneous miracle. A lack of faith would have been her saying, "I choose neither, get out of my room." Yes, I could have ignored her request for option one and went straight for option two, but that is not how God does things. In the Bible, Jesus would approach people and ask them, "Do you want to get well?" I've learned that some people don't want to be healed. They have embraced the sickness or injury as a part of their identity, and they are scared of what life would be like without that in their life. God is gentle and merciful. I always want to try and be like Him. To me, this strategy also shows the person that God cares about the little things. He cares about the choices we make and that each person is involved in the healing. It is something they can think back on and say, "Wow, I asked God to do this specifically, and He did! What else does He want to do in my life?"

Now that we were all in agreement, it was time to pray. I asked her to give me her hand and I prayed in a soft and calm tone. I didn't yell or shake her commanding a 'back breaking devil' to leave her this instant. Volume has nothing to do with authority and power. A simple whisper in Jesus name can break any devil or heal any sickness. We prayed that she wouldn't have to have surgery on her back and that Jesus would touch her spine and bring everything into alignment and give her full strength. After that, I spoke with authority over her back. I prayed, "I command every disc and vertebrae to submit to the commands of Heaven. Spine you be healed and restored right now in Jesus name. I curse inflammation and command it to leave her body right now. I declare at this very moment, that her back is being healed and will be fully restored by God's hand and touch. In Jesus name I pray. Amen."

After I finished the prayer, we all gave the family hugs and went back home. A few weeks later my wife got a phone call from the family. The doctor said her back had made tremendous improvement and no surgery was required. To this day, the family does not say the doctors healed their daughters back, they said Jesus did it. That is what it is all about. It is not about us looking like super Christians with a super anointing. It's about connecting with people, loving them, building relationships, and pointing them to Jesus.

Of course, I know that we don't always have that much time to minister in that way. Sometimes we have three or four minutes to get the job done. If that is the case, I still ask them what they would like for God to do in their life, I share some stories, and then offer to pray. Sometimes people need help through the process. Many times, I will ask the person if they are in pain or if God touched them, would they be able to feel a difference. If they say yes, I tell them that what they are feeling at that moment is a level ten and after I pray for them, I want them to check the area of what we are praying for and see if there is an improvement. Ten would mean nothing happened. Seven or so would be a slight improvement. Five would mean the pain or improvement is half-way, and zero would be total restoration and healing. Don't be afraid to go for it multiple times. I can't even begin to tell you how many times the person's pain dropped to a five the first prayer and I would point out to them that there is progress happening. Using the number scale helps them understand that something is happening which then, increases their faith for us to pray a second time. I would say over ninety percent of the time I pray a second time for someone who had some relief from the first prayer, they were totally healed.

The last thing I will encourage you with is this; Jesus heals bodies so He can get to a person's heart. At the end of the day, our bodies will fail us, and we will die at some point, but our souls live forever. Either our souls will be with Jesus in Heaven or in Hell with the devil for all eternity. Jesus doesn't want a single person separated from Him. He heals to pursue the heart. As people get healed while you pray for them, don't forget about their heart. Make sure they understand who Jesus is and what He has done for them. I usually say something along the lines of this:

"Isn't it amazing that Jesus just healed your body? But guess what? Jesus didn't just pay the price to get you healed. He also paid the price for you to be saved. Every single one of us has sin in our life. Sin is when we do something Jesus wouldn't do, and that sin separates us from Him. There is no way we can perform or do enough good things to go to Heaven. Jesus came to earth and lived a life you and I could not live. He lived a perfect life that you and I could not live. He died a death you and I deserved. Jesus was crucified on a cross taking the punishment for your sin and my sin. But, three days later Jesus rose from the grave. He overcame sin and death and ascended into Heaven and released His Spirit onto the earth to live in those who believe in Him. He didn't just pay the price for your body to feel better. He paid the ultimate price, so you didn't have to go another day without Him. He loves you. So, where are you at with Jesus? Do you want a relationship with Him right now and are you willing to turn away from all the things that separate you from Him?"

If they say yes, lead them in a prayer of salvation. Don't just tell them to go to a church and talk to a pastor. They need YOU right then and there to lead them to Jesus. Scripture says if we confess with our mouth and believe in our heart Jesus is Lord and Savior, He will save us. You don't have to make the prayer complicated. Here is the prayer I typically use when leading someone to Jesus. I have them repeat after me saying:

"Jesus, I believe in You. I believe you are the Son of God. I believe, that you died for my sins and rose from the grave victorious. Jesus, I have sin in my life, and I need your forgiveness. Please, forgive me of my sins and remove any stronghold the devil may have over my life. I forgive those who have hurt me, and I forgive myself for mistakes I have made. Jesus, I ask that you save me and fill me with your Holy Spirit right now. Thank you, Jesus, for loving me and saving me. I declare that I am all yours and you are all mine. In Jesus name. Amen."

After you pray for a person, reassure them of what just

happened. Remind them that their sins are washed away, and they are now in good standing with Jesus. Also, invite them to church or help them find community with other believers. Getting a person connected to the body of Christ is extremely important. It's not hard and yes, YOU CAN DO IT. Remember, it's not about you or your failures or talents. It is about Jesus and what He wants to do, and He wants to use YOU to do amazing things on this earth. Will you let him?

SEVEN

Authority in Christ

Behold, I have given you authority to tread on
serpents and scorpions, and over all the
power of the enemy, and nothing shall
hurt you.
Luke 10:19

LET'S fast forward a little bit. Four years into my relationship with the Lord, in 2015, I was ready and desiring to take on the world. I felt a stirring in my heart and a deep passion to do Gospel Crusades. A Gospel Crusade is basically where you host open air meetings and lead as many people as you can to Jesus. Thousands of people can be in attendance in just a single night. One crusade I did in India had over seventeen thousand people in attendance in just one night of the three night event. My first Gospel Crusade was in Kenya. Through a divine meeting I met a pastor from Kenya who had hosted many crusades, and I knew that I was finally going to have the opportunity to share the Gospel in a way I had always desired. I mean, who wouldn't want to travel halfway around the world and preach the Gospel to thousands of people? How hard could it be? You get on stage, you preach, people get saved, and you call it a night. What problems could occur with an event like this? These were the thoughts I had in my head before going, but when I arrived and as the trip continued, I learned that it literally can be a battle for souls, especially when you preach the Gospel in a town that is known to be home for some of the most powerful witchcraft. This was the town called Kitui, Kenya.

When we arrived in Kitui, we were instructed to not go out at night. We were supposed to stay in our hotels and under any circumstances, not to leave. We were told that the witchcraft in this area was very strong and at night was when the witches were most powerful. Some people even called Kitui "The capital of Kenya for witchcraft". We heard stories of people being cursed and very unusual things happening to them and some even dying. I understood why my host pastor was instructing us to stay in, but I really wanted to be with the people and felt a lot of peace about going out and being in the town. I didn't want to be hiding in my hotel while the witches were running around doing their thing. I wanted to be with the people and show that we were not afraid and that Jesus would protect us.

So, we left the hotel and made our way on foot to the main area of Kitui. Many people that were out stared at us and some would even ask us, "What are you doing out here at night?" We would just tell them that we were hungry and wanted to find a great place to eat. They would tell us which restaurant they recommended and we would pray for them. So many people got healed on the streets while on our little excursions.

We would spend as much time as we could with the people to let them know we love them and truly care about them. While we were in Kenya, the United States President at the time was also in Kenya. The same sex marriage bill had passed in the US and the President was three hours from where we were and was meeting with the Kenyan government. Many of the people in Kitui thought we were sent by the President of the United States to convince people to accept same sex marriage. So, as the days progressed, everything seemed to escalate. We had witches trying to do sacrifices on our crusade grounds, we were summoned by the Governor of Kitui so she could question our motives for being there, we learned a local pastor had his church praying that we would die in a plane crash on the way there, and many of the people in the town were confused as to why we were there. I guess you could say things were getting a little tense.

It was the first night of the crusade. There were about thirteen hundred people in attendance. I was nervous and didn't have much experience with preaching with an interpreter. Needless to say, the night was kind of rough. Seven people came forward to accept Jesus. I'm grateful for the seven that got saved, but out of a crowd of thirteen hundred people....there should have been many more come forward. I realized two things that night. First, my preaching needed to be more bold and authoritative and second, the people were afraid. The people of Kitui had been oppressed by witchcraft for a long time and they needed to see that Jesus was far more powerful. This wasn't the time to just preach the Gospel. This was time to demonstrate it.

The next day we wanted to be out with the people before the crusade started. So we started walking aimlessly down the road in hopes of finding a way to connect with the community. We ended up stumbling across a hospital. I turned and looked at my team and you could tell we all had the same idea. We were going to go pray for the sick. The hospital was full and slightly chaotic. The outside of the hospital served as the waiting room. People were standing outside in hopes of getting in and seeing a doctor. My team and I spread out and began praying for people. I remember praying for a woman who was having intense headaches behind her right eye. After we finished praying, she said the pain left her and left the hospital to go back home. It got to a point where people were getting healed and they didn't need a doctor anymore. The manager of the hospital heard five Americans were outside the hospital, so she came to investigate. I thought we were going to be in trouble since we were causing the hospital to lose business. That wasn't the case at all. She welcomed us to pray for as many people as we wanted, including her. It was such a fun time.

If you want to see miracles and healings, you have to go to the sick and hurting. Miracles require you to put your hands on impossible things and pray with confidence that the impossible is possible. So many people tell me they desire to see miracles but they are not willing to go where a miracle is needed. We live in a world where people are hurting and need help. You don't have to travel to Kenya to see a miracle, you can go to your next door neighbor and see that. Why? Because Jesus Is Still Jesus. Jesus in Africa is the same Jesus in America. He doesn't change. You might be thinking, "But Dennis, what if nothing happens when I pray?" Well, what will happen if you don't pray? Nothing! So, the worst thing that can happen when praying for someone is the same thing we experience all the days we don't pray for people. Nothing. You're not going to hurt the person's faith if you pray and they do not get healed. Actually, it's the exact opposite. When people see that we care for them enough to put ourselves out there to pray for them shows them that they are loved and also increases their faith. Even if the person you pray for is not healed, they will still encounter one thing...love.

So let me get back to this story. It was the second night of the crusade and there were people everywhere. We had approximately 5,000 people in attendance for the crusade. I was excited and nervous. I had never preached in front of so many people and was still getting accustomed to everything. My team and I went into the crowd to meet people, shake hands, and pray for people. It was a lot of fun. Kids would want to touch my hair, teenagers wanted to take pictures, and the adults were either happy to see us or didn't really care too much either way. I knew we had a lot of different opinions and rumors being spread about us in the town so I understood if some people weren't exactly welcoming. After about ten minutes of shaking hands, pictures, and praying for people, a man in a green sweater approached me. His walk was very purposeful and his eyes were locked on me. As he got closer I got the feeling his intentions were not good. I also noticed his eyes were completely black. There was no white to his eyes or eye color, only black. He stopped right in front of me and stuck out his hand, offering a handshake. I knew something was up but still had a tremendous amount of peace. So, I reached out and shook his hand. As we shook hands he began speaking in what seemed to me a very different tongue. I don't know exactly what he was saying but I knew it was a curse. He would bob his head while saying certain things on repeat and it was as if he were pushing "buttons" on my wrist with his fingers that shook my hand. It was like he was touching pressure points on my hand and wrist while speaking curses over me.

I've been familiar with the demonic, but this was brand new to me. I looked around to see what the reaction was from the other people. I could instantly tell everyone was afraid of this man. Many were watching curiously and somewhat anxious to see what would happen next. What seemed like two minutes to process all happened in a matter of seconds. I knew I needed to do something but I didn't know exactly what. So without delay I pulled my hand away respectfully ending the handshake and said, "Bro! Jesus thinks you are amazing. Give me a hug!" I opened up my arms inviting him in for a hug. You should have seen the look on his face. Very puzzled and confused he said, "What?"

"I said, Jesus thinks you're amazing. Now, come give me a hug bro!" I took a step towards him and he stepped back. He had panic written all over his face. I took another step and he stepped away from me once more. I smiled really big at him, "Bro, give me a hug!" I took one last step and he began to run from me. I can't imagine what all was going through his mind. My best guess was he was sent to curse sickness or death on me and instead of me falling over instantly, I was offering peace, love, and a hug! I wasn't thinking much at the moment except, "I'm not letting you get away!" So, I chased him. I literally chased this witch doctor apprentice. We found out later the man was the right hand man to the main witch doctor and I was chasing him across the huge crusade ground in front of thousands of people with my arms wide open yelling, "Wait, you forgot your hug!" It was a rather comical moment now that I think back on it. As I chased him with wide open arms everyone was watching, laughing, and somewhat shocked. He ended up disappearing into a portion of the crowd and by that time it was my turn to get up and preach the Gospel. I thought to myself, "That's the last I'll see of that guy," as I walked to the stage, but I was very very wrong.

Towards the end of my message, I was preparing to do an altar call to ask people if they wanted to give their life to Jesus. I preached with a lot more boldness and authority. I had it in my heart and mind that I wasn't just preaching the Gospel to people, but I was also declaring the Gospel to the demonic principalities in the region. The sun had set during my message and the stars were bright in the sky. I could see the heads of thousands of people all around. The few lights we had lit up the stage and a portion of the field. In front of the stage we had a roped off section so we would have room for people to respond and for us to pray for them. People were pressed up against the ropes not leaving hardly any room at all between each other. I was just about to give the salvation invitation when someone came from the crowd and crossed the ropes. It was him, the man in the green sweater. He had somehow pressed his way through the crowd and crossed the rope and now stood right at the foot of the stage directly in front of me. I looked down at him and could tell something was different. He looked as if he was in a trance of some kind. He was staring at the sky as if he was seeing something we didn't. I looked at the crowd of people and everyone had become unusually quiet. They would change their gaze back and forth from me to him in antici-pation of what was to come. I wasn't sure what was going to happen and I wanted to make sure I didn't give the devil any room to hinder or manipulate the people, especially since we were about to make a call for salvation. I turned to one of my team members and asked him to go down and minister to the man in the green sweater. My friend went down and stood next to him and he put his hand on the witch's shoulder. As soon as my friend touched him, the man shrieked, dropped to the ground, and began convulsing while making some of the most disturbing noises and screams I had ever heard. The man shook violently and began to foam at the mouth.

The entire crowd gasped in shock and became silent. I looked down at this young man and could literally see and hear the devils on him. When he would open his eyes, you could clearly see it wasn't him looking at you. There was such hate and anger in his eyes. The shrieks and roars he would let out sounded like various beasts and torment. It took three people to hold him down so he wouldn't hurt himself or other people. I had never cast the devil out of a person before. Is this really happening? Should I cast it out? Will it work? What if I don't have enough authority? What if this is a really big devil and I am in over my head? It's amazing all the little thoughts and lies that can go through your mind in such moments. I'll be honest with you, I didn't want to address the situation at first. It scared me to be fully honest. I was scared God couldn't use me in that way and also scared of looking like an idiot. I was flooded with doubt and emotions until I felt and heard God speak. I heard the Lord say, "Son, he belongs to me. Set him free." After I heard the Lord say that, I felt a wave of peace cover me like a blanket. As I looked at the man rolling and screaming in torment on the ground, I had a shift in my focus. I no longer saw all the devils that were on him, I saw one of God's creations in need of freedom. I instantly was filled with compassion for him. I had more compassion for him than the worry of looking dumb.

I picked up the microphone to my mouth. I took a deep breath and said in a soft monotone, "In the name of Jesus, I command you devils to let go of this child of God and leave him, now!" Apparently, I made the devils really mad. After I spoke that, the boy seized even more and screamed out in more agony and pain. I was starting to be gripped with fear again. I couldn't stand the fact of seeing this guy hurt like this. For years these devils had been inside of him wreaking havoc on his life. The crowd gasped again and looked at me wondering what I was going to do. Instantly I felt something in my chest. I felt a zeal and righteous anger build up inside of me. I remembered the years of pain I went through personally and how God touched me. I thought of how God set me free and that there was no other alternative. These things had to go and I instantly didn't care if I had to stay there all night with the man praying over him. This was going to end. I picked up the microphone again and with a more stern and authoritative tone I said, "Devils, I said LET HIM GO NOW, in Jesus name. You stop hurting him, you leave him, and you never return." The man was still shaking on the ground. I remember the zeal rising inside of me more. I slightly stomped on the stage and declared. "I said now, devil. Leave in Jesus name."

All of a sudden the man stopped shrieking and yelling, and stopped moving as if he were dead. He didn't move or make a sound. The entire field of people was silent. I stood on the stage looking down at the lifeless body in the green sweater. I seriously had the thought that maybe the devils killed him. Remember, this was my first time to ever cast devils out of a person, and it was in front of five thousand people. A few seconds went by that felt like forever and suddenly the man's eye shot wide open and he inhaled deeply. I could see the white in his eyes along with a beautiful brown color. The ushers brought him up to his feet and he had huge tears rolling down his cheeks. I instantly dropped the microphone and knelt down in front of him. I grabbed the sides of his head and spoke identity and blessing over his life. The Holy Spirit totally took over at that moment. I don't remember what I said, but whatever it was, it broke all of the torment. Years of pain were coming out of him and rolling down his cheeks in the form of tears. The worship team started singing to help the moment.

I looked into the man's eyes and asked, "What do you want?" The man finally looked into my eyes and said, "I want Jesus." I jumped off the stage and gave him the biggest hug I could give a person. While I hugged him I led him through the prayer of salvation. (Many people from Kenya can speak English.) After we said the prayer together I took his hand and put it high in the air and yelled, "Hallelujah." The crowd of people erupted in praise. I got back up on the stage and asked if anyone else would like to give their life to Jesus. More than half the crowd raised their hands. The night before seven people got saved and now close to two thousand five hundred people are giving their life to Jesus. Why? Because they saw that Jesus was more powerful than the witchcraft that has been oppressing them and putting fear in their hearts.

People have to see that Jesus still has the power over the enemy. God has given us all authority in Him. It's not about gifting or being a well known speaker. It is about knowing and connecting with Jesus. He is the one who gives us the authority. We don't earn it. Jesus functioned in three ways while on the earth; information, demonstration, and authority. Jesus clearly said who He is, He demonstrated who He is, and took authority over the devil numerous times. It's not about saying the "right" prayer, it's about loving Jesus and the person who needs freedom. We have to come to a place in our hearts where we love Jesus and the people around us more than the worry of looking dumb, being rejected, and failing.

As you can tell in all of these previous stories, I had no idea what I was doing. I wasn't very educated in many of the things God has done in me and through me. It is important to remember that academically knowing the Bible is not what God intended. Having God's Word in your mind and not in your heart is a dangerous thing. We are all called to relationally know what the Bible says and to relationally know Jesus. True wisdom, knowledge, and understanding is for the heart. God doesn't speak academically, he speaks to the heart. Our minds can not fully grasp the things of God, meaning, our four pound brain cannot fit the fullness of God inside of it. We have to let go of the analytical portion of our minds and open up to Jesus with our hearts. I didn't spend four to eight years in seminary. I spent time with Jesus and had some really good people in my life.

When I read God's Word, I'm not reading to learn how to win an argument or to support a theology I think I have. I read it with the intention of holding hands with Jesus and allowing Him to show me what His Word says. I am no one special. I'm just a guy who has been rescued by Jesus and willing to let Him use me. People often tell me, "Dennis, you could die on one of these trips! Is that a price you are willing to pay?" My response is always the same. "I wrote that check a long time ago. In my eyes, I'm already dead. I don't exist for myself anymore. I exist for Him. My life is in His hands and when He wants me to come home, I will. Not one second later or earlier."

I guess the best way to finish this chapter is with this statement. 'It's not about WHAT you know, it is about WHO you know.' If you want to move in authority, power, and love, there is only one thing you need to do: spend time with Jesus. It's not about what you know or don't know. It's all about Him. The biggest thing is, we need to remove ourselves from the equation. What we can do, can't do, know, or don't know doesn't matter. What matters is getting to know the beautiful person of Jesus and doing what He did.

EIGHT

Fruit is a Weapon

So as to walk in a manner worthy of the Lord,
   fully pleasing to him, bearing fruit in every
   good work and increasing in the knowledge
   of God.
Colossians 1:10

ONE THING I preach on a lot is the fruit of the Holy Spirit. We are
all called to live in love, joy, peace, patience, kindness, goodness,
faithfulness, gentleness and self control. Over the years I feel like
God has taught me many things about these beautiful fruits. We
literally have the invitation to think, feel and act the same way
Jesus does in Heaven. Even while we are here on this earth facing
many different challenges and difficulties, it is still our inheritance
as followers of Christ to be as He is. We can walk through persecu-
tion and still live in love. We can be surrounded by depressing
things and still be filled with joy. We can be immersed in chaos
and yet be unshaken with peace. I had to learn early in my rela-

tionship with God that the fruit of the Spirit is far more than just emotions. When we function in the fruit of the Spirit, we manifest the characteristics of God Himself.

Anybody can have these emotions on a good day or when everything is going the way that they want it, but what about the days when nothing is going your way? I once heard someone say that the best fruit grows in the worst soil. In other words, the times that the fruit is going to be revealed the most is usually the times that are the worst. The situation you are in serves as a backdrop to elaborate on the fruit that is coming from your life. Manifesting the fruit of the Spirit is proof of access and intimacy with Jesus Himself.

What I learned later in my relationship with God is that the fruit of the Spirit is also a weapon. This weapon is very dangerous and traumatizing to the enemy. You will recall the story I told earlier about the man in Mexico while I was on vacation. Love became my weapon at that time. Love stripped down everything that the enemy had put on that man's life. We have to understand that the most powerful Christians are not the ones who can memorize the whole Bible, attend church more than anyone else, say all the right things, or do all the right things at the proper time. It's not even about our giftings that make us powerful.

I will say this, our gifts do help articulate the power of God that we move in but if we do not resemble Jesus in every situation we have surrendered our power and accepted a lower form of being. When we see the scriptures of the full armor of God: the belt of truth, the breastplate of righteousness, feet shod with the readiness that comes from the gospel of peace, the shield of faith, the helmet of Salvation, and the sword of the Spirit, all of these items point to one thing, and that is Jesus. The most powerful Christians are the ones that know, love, are willing to be changed by Jesus and do what He tells them to do. At the time, I did not know that. It was yet another lesson that I had to learn on the mission field of life. Allow me tell you a story of how I saw joy take out a devil.

IT WAS my fourth trip to the Philippines. We were in the southern-most part of the Filipino islands in a village called Margos. This was an amazing little fishing village. The unique thing about this area was that there were over 30 churches in the surrounding villages and no one had come and put on an event like we were going to. We were given permission to set up a stage in a certain area in the village and ended up having over 800 people in atten-dance. At this point we had already been preaching all day and it was time for our impartation service at night. We had a long day of meetings and saw a lot of people get set free and saved, and we were ready to lay hands on 800 people and release the glory of God on their lives.

For the sake of organizing, we divided the people up into different groups and had each group come to the middle of the floor and the pastors and myself would go down the line laying hands on every single person. Some people may think laying hands on 800 people would be very exhausting. Honestly, I thought so as well but once you started seeing God touch the lives of beautiful people, you had this energy inside you that could allow you to go all night. I remember this young boy who was probably around 12 years old came up to me and he was dragging his left leg and holding his left arm as he stood in front of me. The translator told me that he had been paralyzed for quite some time on the left side of his body, that part of his neck was paralyzed, as well as part of his shoulder, elbow, wrist, hip and parts of his leg down to his ankle and toes.

I began laying hands on different areas of his body commanding the feeling to come back and nothing was happening. I sat there for a minute wondering what I was supposed to do and I heard the Lord tell me, "Son, the problem is not his body. He has an injury to his brain. Pray for the right side of his brain." That made sense because the right side of the brain controls the left side of the body and the left side of the brain controls the right side. I told the young man through the translator that I was going to put my hand on his head and pray for him. The young man agreed and I put my hand on the right side of his head and as I prayed in Jesus' name. All of a sudden the glory of God consumed this incredible young man. He ended up being so overwhelmed by the power of God that he could not stand and as he laid there on the ground I could see that parts of his body were shaking uncontrollably. The parts that were shaking were the ones that were previously paralyzed. I could see his neck muscles twitching, his arm muscles, his fingers, and twitching all the way down his leg.. He was totally consumed by the glory of God. I felt the need to stay near him while the other pastors laid hands on the others. The young man was on the ground for only just a few minutes and he finally rose back up to his feet. I asked him if he was okay and with big tears in his eyes he told me that he could feel everything on the left side of his body. I gave him the biggest hug I could give a person and he ended up walking off the floor with no limp whatsoever. I was so amazed. I literally got to see with my own eyes a young man who was paralyzed on the left side of his body be consumed by the power of God and get up and be totally set free, restored, and healed.

This was just the warm up of the night. There were so many

supernatural things that were happening that night that I couldn't keep up with them. Everywhere I turned there were supernatural things happening. There were creative miracles, healings, signs, wonders, and deliverance. It was as if heaven just poured out over those people. It was like heaven itself stepped down and dwelled among the people that night. As the night went on, the presence of God grew more intense. There were times I was having trouble standing. I had to have someone follow me around to make sure I didn't fall out in the glory of God.

Finally, we got to our last group of people and the last group was the young adults. These were young people from the ages 12 to 20. As we called the group forward I could see the excitement in their eyes in anticipation of what was about to happen. This group of young people had been sitting and watching, waiting patiently for their turn to be touched by God. It was the heaviest presence I have ever felt in my life so far. We began laying hands on these young adults and praying over them for Jesus to touch their hearts and for them to be filled with the power of God. The anointing got so strong in that place that all I had to do was wave my hand in front of people and the glory of God would consume these young people. I made my way to about the third row of people, I noticed this young girl. I could tell immediately that she was in a lot of pain and needed freedom. It seemed like she was just almost disconnected from what was happening around her. She had this blank stare with her hair hanging over her eyes. As soon as I approached her she began to manifest devils. She fell to the ground and began screaming and clawing uncontrollably. She also began sweating profusely. It was as if her skin was on fire. I started to take authority over all the spirits that were hindering her and one by one they began to come out, but these things weren't coming out without a fight. They were being very stubborn and very distracting. Every time they would begin to try and take over her senses I would have to command them to stop in Jesus' name. I would have to call the young woman by her name and command her in Jesus name to regain control of her soul. Once she gained control we were able to walk through repentance and freedom. After about fifteen minutes of working with her, we casted out over eleven demons, but there was still one more left and this one wasn't going without a fight. By this time, she had become the main attraction of the entire event. We literally had over 40 people surrounding this young girl to pray and intercede in Jesus' name. The spirit would try to do different things to get us to give up. Sometimes the devil would try the intimidation tactic causing her to scream and claw and other times it would make her go silent to try to convince us that it had left. But as soon as I would say Jesus it would come right back to the surface. Each time we said come out in Jesus' name it would not. At that point, lies would start forming in my mind. I would start thinking that I wasn't good enough to cast this last one out of her or that the devil is way bigger than me and I'm just not Christian enough to cast this out. I also began having all kinds of religious thoughts in my head like maybe I should have read my Bible more before that event or maybe I'm not gifted enough to be able to do this. I wondered if I should have fasted more before the event. It's amazing all the different little thoughts that will intrude in your mind during the most powerful moments.

As all of those thoughts were rushing through my mind, I knew for certain that those were lies but I want to be honest with you. I was running out of ideas and I didn't know what else to do. I tried just about every technique that I knew to do. Little did I know that God was about to do something incredible. All of a sudden joy erupted throughout the whole area. So many people began getting filled with the Spirit of joy all around us. I remember seeing people laughing so hard with tears in their eyes. But these tears weren't tears of defeat or shame; it was just tears of absolute joy. Some of their laughs were so deep that I thought their stomach muscles were going to explode. As the joy erupted it began to spread to other people. All attention had been put on Jesus at that moment. No one was focused or worried about the devil that didn't want to come out of this girl. All of our attention was on Him. It was amazing watching everyone's focus go from concerned about what was going to happen or what might not happen to worshiping our loving God. During this amazing point of worship the young girl on the ground sprung up to her feet. Many people gathered around her to help hold her up. It looked as if her body was convulsing up and down like she was doing a knee bend and then standing straight up. You could immediately tell that this demonic oppression in her life was starting to lose its grip but it still wasn't leaving. People around her put their hands on her as they continued to worship God. You could see in her eyes that she was at times regaining her consciousness and then the devil would take back over. I became curious if she was feeling all of this or was aware of anything that's happening. I was getting mad that this thing had not come out of her yet and concerned it was going to hurt her. So there I was face to face with this girl during this most intense spiritual battle I have ever seen.

There were people all around and I was asking God what to do when suddenly one of the pastors came moving through the crowd. Earlier she was hit with the spirit of joy and she was laughing hysterically. I remember talking to her the next day about what I'm telling you and she said that her stomach was so sore that she could barely move. But as she came through the crowd of people she walked right up to the girl who was manifesting. The girl's gaze set on the pastor and when they locked eyes she began manifesting more, but all the pastor did was laugh and point. Literally the pastor pointed her finger right in the face of this girl who was manifesting a devil and all she did was laugh in this most amazing joy. I had never seen anything like this in my life. I didn't know what to say. I didn't know what to do, so I just kept my mouth shut and did nothing. I had spent over 30 minutes trying to cast devils out of this girl. I had said what I knew to say. I had prayed what I knew to pray and I did not know what to do. I stood there watching this pastor be consumed by joy in pointing at this devil and laughing hysterically.

For those who didn't know what was going on in the situation it would look like this mean pastor is making fun of this woman for having problems but what was really happening was a spirit of joy was stripping the devil's power off of this beautiful girl. After about two minutes of this happening the young girl let out a huge exhale and collapsed. As she laid on the ground you could tell the one final demon had finally left her. Many people began celebrating and others began praying over her for the Holy Spirit to come and fill her life. Only a few moments went by until her eyes shot wide open and she was totally free and back in control. What surprised me though is that she was puzzled by what had happened. She was asking everyone what had happened. And all of her friends were crying and hugging her and just telling her that she had been set free. When her friends told her that she had been set free she immediately broke down in tears and hugged her friends. We ushered her to the side so she could sit down in a chair and collect her thoughts for a bit. There were a lot of things going through her mind and she knew everything had just changed in her life. So I walked away to give her some space and to handle the rest of the service. Her friends also rejoined the service to give their friend time to recover. We announced that we were going to play one final song and were going to celebrate everything Jesus had just done. But right before the song started the crowd erupted in absolute praise and excitement. Many of the young adults were screaming at the top of their lungs jumping up and down. I gazed into the crowd to see what was going on and I noticed that the young girl had joined back with the rest of the group but there was something very different about her. Her face and her complexion had totally changed. The only way I could recognize her was because of the clothes that she was wearing. She was literally so changed in her heart that it changed her physical features. She had a glow about her. For years these demonic personalities had been hurting and manipulating her and confusing her to the point of changing her physical looks. But what took years for the devil to do Jesus undid in just thirty minutes.

Not only that, God was so graceful and kind to her that he didn't allow her to remember or feel what was happening while she was being delivered. That was the night I saw joy take out a devil. Many people ask me when I tell this story why it didn't work when I would command the devil to leave in Jesus name. People ask me if I had lost faith in the moment or if I didn't have a full understanding of my authority. I think it was because God was wanting to show me something very important. I think God used that night to show me how important and how powerful joy can be in the life of a Christian. Joy is much more than a feeling of happiness. Joy is a surrendered focus to the lover of our souls. It is the faith and the understanding that no matter what happens in our lives that God is in control and that there is no spirit that can take away what God has given us. Joy is accepting the full embrace of God's presence in our hearts. Joy is the moment where we live on earth like we will in heaven. Joy is when the pleasure of God manifests in our hearts and it is dangerous to the enemy. Joy protects our minds from the lies and manipulations of evil. It keeps us in this place a fulfillment to the promises that God has for us. Joy is supported by love and peace and should be found in every single one of our hearts. Imagine what joy could do in your life? Also, you need to ask yourself the question: Why is the devil constantly contending against you and trying to steal your joy?

You know it is much easier to fight someone if they don't have a weapon. If you can take that person's weapon from them while you have your own it's a lot easier to defeat them. That is why Satan tries to lure Christians into a state of misery and chaos and turmoil. Satan tries to keep us in this place of disappointment in past failures, anxious about the unknown future, and worried about current difficulties. Satan whispers into the hearts of Christians telling them what they are not to keep them from understanding who they really are. The devil knows if we show up to the fight fully armed and ready with all the things that heaven has for us, he has no fighting chance. So he uses intimidation and fear as a strategy to keep us from showing up for the fight. I think also the devil tries to make things very complex. I think he tries to put it in our head that everything has to be very complex and very difficult when it can actually be simple and childlike.

There may be hard days of being a Christian, but knowing Jesus should always be simple. Being filled with His love and joy and peace is a free gift that God gives, and this free gift can totally dismantle the strategies of hell. So the question is, how do you get your joy back? How do you regain something that may have been missing for years? Some of you may be reading this and think, 'I don't even remember the last time I've been joyful and I can't even remember the last time I've been excited about anything.' I think a lot of times we miss out on joy because we're asking ourselves the question of what we need to do to regain joy, but it's not about what we do, it's about what Jesus already has done.

When we change our focus from ourselves to Jesus we are then able to behold and grasp who he is. When all of our attention is set on him we can then inherit the very nature of who He is in our souls. I'm reminded of the story of Martha and Mary in the Bible. Mary sat at the feet of Jesus while Martha went around the house taking care of many things that needed to be taken care of, but Martha grew mad at Mary. Martha ended up going to Jesus and demanding him to tell Mary to get up and help her. But Jesus said, "Martha you are worried and concerned about many things and Mary has chosen what is greater and it will not be taken from her."

Mary chose joy, fulfillment, and intimacy while Martha chose work, performance, and busyness. We can see in the Bible that Martha is stressed and anxious. But what is Mary doing? She is sitting at the feet of Jesus and enjoying him. That is the ultimate source of joy. The way to access joy in our lives is to be at his feet. It is to pursue his presence on a daily basis no matter what is going on. Even if life is chaotic and you have hardly any time for yourself, you still find time to be with him. That is ultimately what Jesus wants. Jesus wants a friendship and relationship with us and when we pursue that we are filled with the love and joy and peace that he freely offers.

NINE

Healed of PTSD

*Consider it pure joy, my brothers, when you
encounter trials of many kinds, because you
know that the testing of your faith develops
perseverance. Allow perseverance to finish
its work, so that you may be mature and
complete, not lacking anything.*
James 1:2-4

GROWING up I had a very adventurous life. I enjoyed being
outdoors and sports. I trained in martial arts ever since I was a
little kid, and was fascinated by it. I ended up achieving blackbelts
in different martial art disciplines and fought in numerous tourna-
ments including MMA cage fighting. I liked the physicality and
the challenges it presented to me. I also played football, raced dirt
bikes, and rode four-wheelers for fun. All of these are very fun
activities, until you end up with six concussions like I did. In my
life I received two concussions from combat sports, two from foot-

ball, one from supercross racing, and another one from poor choices on a four-wheeler. When you are young you think you're invincible, that nothing bad can happen to you. As you get older you start to see the signs of wear on your body and your mind from the things of your past. There were also some points in my young life that could best be described as stressful. In junior high, I would have to talk my friend out of killing himself over the phone every night, for six months. I wasn't the most popular kid in school at the time, and as I shared with you earlier, I was my worst enemy. So anytime something bad would happen in my life, I would be consumed with the thoughts of how that situation was my fault. Martial arts came in handy tremendously for me because it was my outlet of stress. So I guess you could say fighting has always been a big part of my life. I've either always been fighting for something or against something.

In our walk with Jesus, there are two battles we will always face. We will face the battle of taking ground and the battle of keeping ground. We will have breakthroughs of freedom and healing, and that is the battle of taking ground. After that comes another battle. Once we have a specific breakthrough or victory in our lives, we then have to learn how to maintain that ground and keep it. That is where the battle of keeping ground comes into play.

Many times as Christians, we are great at gaining ground, but we struggle in keeping. For an example, we may experience brief freedom from an addiction or a circumstance, but after only a few weeks or months, we end up right back where we started. Why? Because we knew how to take the ground but we did not know how to keep it. It is through God's grace and mercy that helps us win the first battle.

The second battle however, is attained through obedience,

surrender, humility, and the fear of the Lord. I'm not saying this in a religious way, I mean it in a relational way. In order for a marriage to work both people have to be willing to be obedient, to be surrendered to one another, to be humble before each other, and to deeply respect one another. That is what I mean by how we win the second battle. In order to keep the ground we have gained, we have to stay in a constant place of surrender and adoration to the Lord. I learned this lesson early in my Christian walk, but I've discovered that there are many layers of learning a certain lesson.

We have to understand that there are many realms of wisdom and revelation. God will take us through very unique processes to teach us the deeper things of who He is and who He calls us to be. During these times you can be certain that the devil will be telling you that you have been forgotten, that God is judging you, and that you were never free in the first place. You can rest assured that the reason we go through those types of seasons is because Jesus loves us, cares for us, and is equipping us in deeper levels to be more like Him and who we are called to be. I had to learn this lesson when I got diagnosed with PTSD.

Let me make myself very clear. Jesus did not give me PTSD. This condition came from physical and emotional trauma. He didn't give it to me, but He did provide a way out. I want to share this story with you, because this may be something you are dealing with personally, or you may know someone who is dealing with this exact same diagnosis as well. Mental disorders are nothing to joke about. Mental disorders such as PTSD , bipolar, schizophrenia, split personalities, ADD and ADHD are very real and painful. I would never wish one of these conditions on a person. But, I tell you these things not to discourage you, but to let you know that there is a way to be free. His name is Jesus.

In 2017, I stepped into the cage to compete one last time. My opponent and I ended up runners up for the best fight of the night. As soon as the bell rang for the first round, he and I went after each other. It was one of the most intense matches I had ever been in. The fight ended in the second round. I ended up with a concussion and he ended up with a broken hand. Those three things I listed should tell you how the fight ended.

After the fight, I was backstage with the guy that I just finished fighting. I congratulated him on his victory and ended up praying for him and his marriage. We talked for quite some time after our fight. For months we would message each other on Facebook and check in on each other. We would let each other know how life was going and if we ever thought of getting back in the ring. Some of my closest friends have been guys I've competed against.

About six months after the fight I ended up having trouble with my thoughts and sleep. I was having horrible nightmares at night. It was as if my mind was caught in a loop of repeating certain failures in my life. Random times of the day, I would become very tired and depressed. I would pray, worship, and I would get in God's word and read, but was struggling to break free of this unusual cycle I found myself in. Many mornings I would wake up and feel like somebody punched me in the gut and that someone stole the fire in my mind. I was having anxiety attacks for no reason. I could be going for a peaceful walk, not thinking of anything bad, and just start hyperventilating and panicking. There were days the only thing I could do was lay on the floor and cry for hours. I don't want to elaborate much more, but I will tell you this, I had somehow become convinced that people's lives would be better if I was gone. It was a thought I could not shake.

The whole time I knew who I was In Christ. I knew Jesus was for me. I knew what He did for me. I knew that He loved me outrageously. I knew that I had a transformed mind, but for some reason, I couldn't let it manifest through my soul. I was scared to tell people about what I was feeling and how I was doing.

I finally got the courage to tell one of my friends at the time. I explained to him how I was feeling and what I was going through. After I shared as much as I felt I needed to share, he responded with this, "You are not believing in your promises. You are not praying hard enough. You are being lukewarm and you need to put on your big boy pants and deal with this." He said, "You just need a renewed mind, so fix it and stop feeling sorry for yourself."

I'm not gonna lie, that conversation shattered me. I knew that something was wrong, but I was also wondering if he was right. Was I just not being disciplined enough? Is there a hidden sin in my life? Am I not being a good enough Christian? Did I bring all of this onto myself? What was I gonna do? That was a question I did not know the answer to. After some time I finally decided to go see a doctor. I sat down in his office and began to tell him about all the symptoms that I was having and my medical background. At that appointment, the doctor prescribed me medicine to begin the treatment process for symptoms of PTSD. When he mentioned PTSD I asked, "But doctor, I've never been in the military, nor have I been a first responder of any kind. So why would you say that I need to be treated for PTSD?"

He explained that more civilians are diagnosed with PTSD than military and first responders. PTSD comes from physical and emotional trauma. These traumas literally rewire your brain in a different way. They can hinder your serotonin, epinephrine levels, and your dopamine levels. When those levels are off, your brain becomes unstable. You have a strong mind but the problem is your brain. Your brain is an organ that can get sick just like any other organ. He shared that the brain represents hardware and your mind is like software. He told me, "Your software is great but it is no longer compatible with the hardware. It's like trying to watch a 3D movie on a 1950s television." My mind was fine. It's the brain that needed to be fixed.

I had never thought of it that way before. I always thought that your mind and your brain are the exact same things. I had been spending all of my time praying to think in a different way even though I knew exactly how to think. But what I needed was a physical healing of my brain.

After that, months went by and I had been on medication for a few months. It took us a while to find the right medication that worked for me. The first four had the opposite effect of what I was needing, but we finally found what worked best. The doctor determined that the six concussions I had accumulated in my life had caused my brain to produce very little dopamine. Dopamine helps with your reward system, drive, ambition, and many other things. The medicine was to help that and also another medication to help with anxiety.

During that time I had applied to attend a week long training course at a well known ministry in Florida. They were hosting a school of evangelism, where they were going to train 100 evangelists for an entire week and I deeply wanted to be a part of it. However, I didn't know they were having the class until about a month before it was going to start. Signups were already past due but I applied anyway. By the grace of God I was accepted into the school and I was on my way to Florida.

At that school were some of the most amazing men and women of God I have ever met in my life. The team of teachers poured into us nonstop. We would start early in the morning and wouldn't make it back to our hotels until later in the evening. Our days were filled with training, prayer, worship, and impartation.

During the third night while in Florida, I had a dream. In the dream, I had gotten out of the bed I was physically sleeping in and walked to the bathroom to take my anxiety medication. When I picked up the bottle in my dream, I noticed that my pill container was extremely heavy. Curiously, I opened up the pill container and looked inside. Instead of seeing all of my pills that would assist me with anxiety, I saw a hurricane of water swirling inside the pill container. In the dream it looked like a category five hurricane right there in my pill container. As I looked closer in the dream I saw that the pills were in the water dissolving. I panicked and poured the water out and noticed when the water was poured out it was clear without any diluted substances from the medication. I sharply woke up from the dream and sat up straight in my bed. I checked my phone and it was around 3:00 AM the next morning. I was confused if that was something that really happened or if it was a dream. I asked the Lord, "Jesus, what just happened?" And I heard the Lord tell me, "Son, it ends today." I was all of a sudden engulfed by His peace. His peace was so heavy that I fell asleep immediately.

I woke up the next morning remembering everything that had happened in the middle of the night. I got myself ready, had break-fast, and put my books, materials, and medication in my bag for the day. I drove over to the training facility to start another day of school. I was attentive to everything that the trainers were talking about, but I also had this underlying anticipation for what I was hoping was going to happen.

One of the teachers that we had was a heart surgeon. He was talking to us about evangelizing in the workplace. This man was telling us stories about all the people that had been raised from the dead on his surgery table. As he spoke you could feel the love of God move in the room. Suddenly, I heard the Lord speak to me, "Son, he is about to ask people to come forward for prayer. If you take your medicine down there with you, I will heal you."

I was slightly embarrassed to be an evangelist, to be a child of God, in the room that I was in, and have that kind of medicine in my bag. I was afraid that everyone else's response would be the same as my previous friend, but when I heard the Lord tell me that, I decided to be obedient. I reached down, unzipped my bag, and took the medication into my hands. As soon as I did, the teacher said, "Hey, do any of you need healing? Come down here right now and let's take care of it."

I immediately jumped up and ran down to where he was. With pills in my hand and tears in my eyes I was ready to be healed and set free. I was surrounded by many other people who were needing healing in their bodies or in their hearts. The teacher began praying for individuals and the power of God consumed every single one of them. As the teacher got closer to me I began shaking. He stood in front of me and he noticed the pills in my hands. He pointed at them and asked, "What it was?" I explained that it was medicine prescribed for my recent diagnosis of PTSD. The teacher peered into my eyes with what seemed like minutes but was actually only a second. As I looked back into his eyes I could see compassion and sincerity, and he said, "No." Then he put his hand on my head and said, "Jesus!"

The next thing I knew I was on the floor. It felt like I was hit by a lightning bolt. I remember laying on the ground with the feeling of electricity in my brain. It was a very different feeling. My brain felt like a flower that was beginning to blossom. This whole time I felt like my brain was condensed and matted down, but when that man prayed for me and when Jesus touched me, it was as if everything in my brain opened back up and was restored to its original place. Once I was able to regain control of my body, I stood to my feet and went back to my seat.

At my seat was another student who was standing at my seat waiting for me . The spirit of joy had consumed him and he was laughing with that deep gut laugh that I'd seen before. As I got close to him he reached over, grabbed me, and pulled me in for a big bear hug. While he held me close he then began prophesying and telling me everything that I had been through for the past two years. He said every hardship and every challenge I had experienced, in order of them happening. He told me, "Dennis, the reason why God told me these things is so you would believe me when I tell you what I'm about to tell you."

He then proceeded to tell me something that I felt like God had been telling me for years but I thought it was too good to be true. I sat there for the rest of the meeting with my shirt soaked from tears and the feeling of electricity surging through my brain. That feeling lasted for well over an hour and since that day I have never needed to take medication again. All of the thoughts, heaviness, nightmares, sense of worthlessness left and have never come back. God used that teacher to set me free of what was hurting me the most.

I remember that night sitting in my hotel room collecting my thoughts from everything that had happened during the class. I couldn't help but cry thinking of what Jesus just did for me and how I had made that condition bigger than God. I didn't think that there was any way out of that, because you hear people talk about how horrible these conditions are and they are right. No one deserves to go through any type of mental disorder, but it is not incurable. There is a way to be free, and it's available through Jesus.

You know in the Bible there was a man who was possessed with over 2000 demons. The man lived in the tombs and would cut himself at night to try to make himself numb to the agony that he was living in. One day, when Jesus stepped onto the beach where the man lived, there was no devil or hindrance that could keep the man from falling at the feet of Jesus and being set free. Jesus did it for him, Jesus did it for me, and Jesus can do it for you as well. I'm not making light of the situation of what people are facing, but I am saying, there is a way to freedom. Jesus is still Jesus.

There is no sickness or disorder that is bigger than Him. He can heal and He wants to heal. He doesn't want his kids living in such conditions. As some people read this they will think, "Yeah, but you don't know what I've seen or what I've been through. If you had gone through what I had gone through you probably wouldn't get healed."

It's never about what we did or what we didn't do. It's about who Jesus is. Also we need to remember not to make our lives all about comparisons. Warfare is warfare and pain is pain no matter what the level or intensity. I know that there are people that have had to make a life changing decision in a fraction of a second with intense pressure all around them. I know that people have had to choose life or death in the midst of chaos, but those decisions do not have a right to haunt them for the rest of their life. What happened yesterday does not have the right to dictate, harm, or manipulate today and tomorrow. It is God's greatest desire for His children to be free and if we come to Him and open up our lives and our hearts to Him, He will do it.

I remember the Bible verse that says freely you've been given so freely give. That is something that I have felt led to do. Since Jesus set me free from those symptoms, I go out and pray for others to be free of the exact same thing. We have to understand that the things that the devil meant to destroy us with become our permission of redemption in heaven. What was meant to destroy us becomes our weapon. For those who have been set free of lust now have permission to go set other people free from lust. For those who were set free of depression have permission to go set other people free from depression. What the devil meant for harm God turns for good. So if you are struggling with a mental disorder I would like to pray for you right now. As you read this prayer I need you to understand something. It's not about what you have to do to earn this answered prayer, it's not about being a good enough person, or a strong enough attitude. Your only focus that you need in this prayer is God's love for you. So before you read this prayer, spend some time just thinking, pondering, and receiving God's love and when you are ready, read this prayer out loud.

Jesus, thank you for loving me. Thank you for all that you have done in my life. Jesus, I ask that you heal my brain of every mental disorder and symptom that comes with it right now in Jesus name. Lord restore my levels in my brain. Restore the receptors in my brain. Remove every hindrance, every sickness, and every barrier right now in Jesus name. I declare that my symptoms are not my identity. These symptoms are not who I am. I am who you say I am. You gave me an identity long before anyone had an opinion or before the symptoms attached to me. So I declare right now, that by the blood of Jesus Christ, that I am healed, that I am restored and that these symptoms have no part of me. I declare my brain healed, my mind healed, and my heart healed in Jesus name. Amen

TEN

Prophecy in the Operating Room

*Be joyful in hope, patient in affliction, faithful in
prayer.*
Romans 12:12

ONE OF MY goals in this book is to be very vulnerable and transparent with you. This book isn't intended to be a resume of all of my victories in ministry. This book is meant to glorify Jesus, and Him alone. I want to share a story with you of a season that I've had to endure that was very challenging and hard for me. In this season, I had a lot of doubts and I also had a lot of people questioning me. I wish I could tell you that I handled this situation with ease, but this was definitely one of the times of my life where I could relate to the man in scripture who said, "I believe. Help my unbelief."

There were many days and nights of pain. There was frustration and many conversations with God saying, "Lord, if there is anything good that can come from this please allow it." If you had or will have to endure any type of hardship, this is an encouragement to you.

A few months after having my encounter with God and being healed of PTSD symptoms, I was asked to help lead a team to Nepal and go backpacking through the Himalayan Mountains. I had done a trip like this previously and absolutely loved it. It was a unique experience of getting to backpack through some of the most beautiful mountains in the world, meet the most wonderful people, and preach the gospel to those who had never heard of Jesus in their life. When I received the offer to go to Nepal to do the same type of trip, I did not hesitate to say yes.

The hardest part about these trips is the physical requirements. The trip is very taxing on your body and you have to prepare yourself long before the trip begins. You have to make sure that your body is ready, your mind is ready, your spirit is ready, and that you have all the appropriate gear to take on the mountains. I decided to commit to a rigorous training program in preparation for the trip. I would wear an elevation mask during my intense workouts that would simulate oxygen levels at high altitudes. So not only would I be lifting weights and running, but it would be as if I was doing those workouts on top of a mountain where there was less oxygen. One day while I was doing a workout, I pushed myself a little too far and felt my back pop. I instantly felt pain radiating down my right leg. I dropped my weight and attempted to shake off the pain and then continued on with my workout. I only made it a few more reps and realized that something was very wrong. It felt like I had a knife stuck in my lower back and every time I moved all of my nerves and muscles became extremely irritated.

I tried to fight off the pain as long as I could until finally, I decided I needed to get it looked at. After visiting a specialist, having x-rays, MRI's, and other tests, we discovered that I had a herniated disc in my lower back. In between each of your vertebrae in your spine you have discs. They are basically the cushions between your bones and one of the cushions in my spine had pushed out of place and was rubbing on my spinal cord. The images from the MRI looked like there was a pinky finger sticking out of my spine and hitting my spinal cord. It was a pain I wasn't used to at all. I immediately began praying to be healed. I would put my hands on my back and declare the fire of God, I would fast, and I would rebuke Satan. I prayed every prayer I knew to pray, but I was still hurting. I had numerous friends and ministry leaders lay hands on me and pray for healing with no result. Word had gotten out to many people about my injury and people started asking questions. I had some people tell me that I was not praying hard enough or correctly. Others said I had hidden sin that I needed to deal with. There were also others that said the reason why I didn't get healed was because I didn't have enough faith.

As time went on, I began to get messages, phone calls, emails, and conversations with people that would ask me, "Dennis, if you can go around the world healing people in the name of Jesus, why are you not getting healed? You always say that Jesus is still Jesus, why is Jesus not being Jesus in your own life?" I would assure them by saying, "Just because I'm not seeing what I'm praying for doesn't mean that God is less powerful or less loving. I trust him. I love him. And I know that is all going to work out, and He will get the glory."

I would do my best to not get discouraged, but there were days the enemy would convince me what the people were saying could possibly be true. I started to ponder if I had done something wrong or if I didn't have enough faith. I even had a few people say, "Your insecurity is preventing you from being healed. You really need to let go of your self-hatred and move on." After many days and nights of praying, fasting, declaring, and spiritual warfare, I realized that my focus was off. My focus was on me the entire time, instead of what Jesus wanted and how He wanted to use me during this time of vulnerability. I finally prayed, "Jesus, I trust that even if You don't heal me, You will take care of me. Use me Lord, to be a light. Let people see You in me during this time. I'm not going to allow this injury and the opinion of others to make me silent or doubt what I know is true about You." After praying that, I had peace fill my heart and the religious opinions of other people no longer had influence in my thoughts and heart.

I finally stopped feeling sorry for myself and continued to be the person God created me to be. Even though I had not been healed yet, I didn't stop praying for other people to be healed. As a matter of fact, during the time of my injury, I saw hundreds of people get miraculously healed. In Nigeria, I saw an older man who had crushed his back at a young age get touched and miraculously healed by Jesus when I prayed for Him. I didn't get mad when I saw the man was healed. It filled me with compassion. I understood the pain he had been through and it excited me to see the joy in his eyes. I would think to myself, "Wow, the devil must be getting really frustrated with me that I haven't allowed this injury to stop me from being who Jesus has called me to be.... Let's keep going." My pain became my fuel. I realized that it takes more faith to persevere through a circumstance and continue to contend for the breakthrough of others than to see your own healing. Also, as time went on, I started getting more messages, emails, calls, and conversations from other people. They would say, "Dennis, watching you go through this has encouraged me. You have shown me that feelings don't determine your faith, but His word does. Thank you for showing me that." I was shocked. I didn't realize people were even watching me in that way. I was just trying to not let the pain get the best of me and for the enemy and religious people not get in my head with twisted thoughts and theology. Our lives are a testimony about Jesus.... ESPECIALLY when things are tough. I could see God moving in the situation, but I was not prepared at all for what was going to happen on the day of my surgery.

After many doctor visits, tests, and injections it was time to commit to surgery. I arrived at the hospital early that morning and started going through the preoperative routine. Nurses would ask me over and over again for my name, birthday, and what the doctor was going to be operating on and I was wearing a bright yellow gown with the famous and revealing open back area. After I had been briefed numerous times and signed all the correct papers a new doctor came in and said it was time for my first phase of medicine that would start the sedation process. He called it his little "margarita shot". He told me to give my wife a hug and a kiss if I wanted to, because once he gave me that shot, I was going to start feeling loopy and they would be taking me straight to the operation room. I gave my wife a kiss and he gave me the shot.

I remember being wheeled down a long hallway with doctors and nurses everywhere. It reminded me of high school when I played football. As we would make our way onto the field, people would line up on both sides of the entrance wanting to give us high fives. I was feeling the effects of the "margarita shot" and thought it would be a great idea to try to give high fives to the doctors and nurses as I went by saying, "Jesus loves you."

The last thing I remember was being in the operating room. I had about six people staring at me as they stood around this unusual table, they were about to put me on for surgery. I remember a nurse in purple scrubs starting to reach for me to transfer me to the table and that was it. I was totally out.

I hear the sound of my heart monitor and the voice of two women talking. My eyelids felt like they weighed one hundred pounds each. "Mr. Funderburg, welcome back." One nurse said as I tried to open my eyes to see where I was. After a couple of minutes, I could open my eyes and see that I was in recovery. I finally got my bearings and asked, "How was the surgery?" The nurse said, "Your procedure went exactly as planned."

I then had this odd feeling that I need to ask them this question, "Did it take longer than expected?" The nurses paused and looked at each other briefly with a puzzled stare as if I asked a question I should have known the answer to or that I asked something that was forbidden. Finally, the other nurse said, "Well, we did have about a twenty-minute delay before your surgery started."

"What? What happened?" I said as hundreds of thoughts raced through my brain. Did I do something stupid? Did they drop me? Did the doctor forget what to operate on and need to look it up really quick? What happened?

"Nothing bad happened in there sweetheart, it's just, you wouldn't allow us to start the procedure until you prayed for every single one of us." My eyes lit up and opened wide. "Mr. Funderburg, you don't remember any of that?"

"No ma'am, I don't. All I remember is the nurse reaching for me in the purple scrubs." They both looked at each other again with the same look and the same lady who had been spoken said,

"Honey, I don't know how you did it, but you knew things that were going on in each of our lives that nobody else did and prayed things that we never thought of praying. Some of us in the room couldn't stop shaking and crying."

When she said that I knew things other people didn't, I got worried, "Did I embarrass anyone?" I love the gift of prophecy, but I always want to speak into people from a place of love and hope and was scared that I might have come across as judgmental or accusing.

"Oh no, sweetheart. You were very kind. You were pointing out things in us that we had never seen in ourselves before." I was absolutely shocked. The nurses changed the subject and I continued on with the recovery process. I spent the night at the hospital and couldn't stop thinking about what happened. I was totally sedated, and the Holy Spirit spoke through me to reach His children and express His love. I wish I could tell you everything that happened, what was said, and the fruit of it, but I can't. All I know is that I remained surrendered to Jesus even in the time of pain. I'm not saying God caused my back to be injured, but I know He put every doctor and nurse in place to be in the room that morning so He could use a willing vessel to express Himself to them.

Here is why I share this story, even if you are going through pain, a hard season, and/or enduring doubters around you, God still has a plan and wants to use you for good. He really can take any situation and turn it around for the good of those who love Him. We are not the judge, He is. He is all seeing and all knowing, we are not. Many times, we exhaust ourselves praying and binding things that are actually in the will of God. There are times we need to fight in spiritual warfare and there are times we need to pray and press in, but there are also other times when we need to trust Jesus and allow Him to put us through the work and process He wants us to go through. I have learned that God is more interested in the process than the provision at times. Process helps us develop our character. The Bible says, "Let perseverance finish its work so that we may be complete and not lacking anything." Our character consists of our humility, discipline, and our patience. If our character is not strong, our very giftings can crush us. The Bible also says, "An inheritance gained too early isn't blessed in the end."

Imagine if a man was hired to build an amazing 40 story skyscraper. He was told to build it strong, beautiful, and within budget. The man makes his plans to build the beautiful building. The details and design will be so great that everyone will marvel when they see it, but in order to make the building extra amazing in his design, he needs to cut some corners in the building material. He decides to spend less money on the foundation and structure of the building so that he can invest more in the design. What would happen to the building? It would eventually buckle and come crashing down. It is exactly the same with our character and giftings. If we do not allow God to work on our character, our own giftings can cause us to tumble.

Sadly, in ministry, we have seen powerful and gifted men and women of God step out of ministry because of this. They were greatly gifted but their character couldn't handle it. They lacked humility, discipline, and patience in key areas of their lives and the weight of their gifting was too much for them. That is why it is important to learn perseverance. That is why it is important to have to go through hard seasons at times. That is why sometimes God will say, "Not now." Rather than "Now."

I know that Jesus said, "Everything you ask in my name is yes and amen." We just have to remember that His yes may not look the way we think it should. An example would be, "Jesus, will you please heal me?" Instead of Him responding with what we want, "Yes, be healed, body be restored right now. Ok, go live your life now." He may say, "I will start the healing process, but along the way I'm going to use this to show you more about Me, yourself, and allow your temporary weakness to reveal my Glory."

This is why I am not a huge fan of the "name it and claim it" kind of faith. I know God calls us to prosper but I also believe He has committed us to the process of becoming more like His Son, Jesus. That requires us going through significant changes, and those changes require us to not get every single thing the way we want and how we want it. I will say this though, even in the midst of the pain and hard days, I knew He was still with me. I still had a sense of His presence and peace. Even though I wasn't "feeling" Him, I simply understood He was with me. We have to be a people whose faith exceeds their feelings. The Bible says, "Consider it pure joy, whenever you face trials of many kind, because the testing of your faith produces perseverance." What if we are to consider it pure joy because in the trial, there is a provision, a blessing, a breakthrough, or a piece of who Jesus is, He wants us to discover and make it a part of us?

Father, I trust you with all of my circumstances and troubles. I ask that you use all things to glorify Yourself and for my good. Lord, develop my character to be more like yours every day. Teach me how to see the provision of Heaven in all circumstances. Teach me to have peace in the waiting, joy in humility, love in the discipline, and goodness in the patience. Jesus, I say yes to the process of You making me more like Yourself. Teach me how to recognize what is warfare and what is You. Jesus I give you permission to use my weaknesses for your Glory. In Jesus' name I pray, Amen.

ELEVEN

The only question you need to ask yourself

Set your mind on things above, not on things on
the earth.
Colossians 3:2

SHALL WE CHANGE THE SUBJECT? Travelling to different places around the world, you have the blessing of seeing some amazing things. You can see masses of people get saved in a single moment, crazy manifestations, different encounters with demon possession, angelic encounters, signs, wonders, and beautiful moments when people are filled with the Holy Spirit. I always enjoy it when I see people get saved, healed, delivered, and encounter the Holy Spirit.

Many times, though, I find myself in conversation with people who have yet to have had an encounter with the Spirit of God and are plagued with doubts and questions. I've had many Christians ask me, "How do I know if I have the Holy Spirit? Do I have to fall down? Am I even saved if I have not had that type of encounter? Am I good enough of a Christian to receive Him?"

It's amazing and sad at the same time all the lies we allow to penetrate our hearts and minds that keep us trapped in a lower form of being. We live in a world where in some circles the Holy Spirit is not welcome, some where He is, other circles where the Holy Spirit is mocked or taken for granted, and some circles where the Holy Spirit is an unknown mystery that people have become afraid of. Many times, I've seen people feeding off of their own emotions and call it "Holy Spirit".

I've seen moments where the Holy Spirit will start to move, and leaders quickly shut the meeting down or interrupt the flow because they are afraid of losing control. Then there are the people in the middle of it all, watching other people fall on the ground, flop around, scream in tongues, and then get up and live their life the exact same way as they did before the encounter leaving everyone around them that doesn't quite know the Holy Spirit with more doubts and a lot more questions.

These are the days when God's children need to encounter and know the Holy Spirit the most. In this world of darkness, Christians need to be filled and empowered with the love, grace, and mercy of the Spirit of the living God. Wherever the Holy Spirit is, there is liberty. That means, when the Holy Spirit is around, bondage and oppression cannot exist.

The Bible says the Holy Spirit is our helper, our teacher, and our comforter. That means, in life we are going to need help, won't know what to do, and will be uncomfortable. Sadly, there are many pastors in the world who think their man-made programs can replace the help, teaching, and comfort of the Holy Spirit. No one can help, teach, and comfort like the Holy Spirit can and there are millions of Christians in the world who have yet to experience Him. This is not a pastor bashing chapter. I'm simply stating what I have observed.

This chapter is to share stories that will encourage people to be hungry for the Holy Spirit, because it does not matter of your age, race, religious background, or past. He wants to fill every single heart that will welcome Him in. People are filled with millions of questions in regard to the Holy Spirit, but indeed when it comes to the Holy Spirit, there is only one question you need to ask yourself. ARE YOU HUNGRY?

I won't share which country this was in or the name of the individual in respect of his privacy and for his protection. I was out internationally and had visited a church. The amazing people honored me by giving me a seat up front during worship. I began to reflect on the Lord and continue to prepare my heart to preach. Instead of focusing on the message, the Holy Spirit started pointing people out to me, or what I call, "highlighting". What happens is, when the Holy Spirit wants you to share something with a person or do something, He will cause that person to catch your attention. They may not be doing anything out of the ordinary to do so, but your attention is drawn to them and He keeps bringing your attention back to them. Anyway, the Holy Spirit had highlighted three individuals to me and gave me a specific word about all three of them. He told me what their role was in the church and how their past had prepared them. Once it came my time to preach, I asked the three men to join me on stage. I prophesied over the first two men and it was beautiful and powerful. It was the third person the Lord spoke to me about that I want to share with you.

This is what I spoke over him, "Sir, you have been asking and wondering if you really are welcome in the body of Christ. The devil has been attempting to fill you with doubt and shame to keep you from where you truly belong. Not only do you belong to the body of Christ, you are an important part of the body of

Christ. You are called to be a pillar for the church. You are called to serve as the backbone of the church, to maintain her posture and integrity. You are called to be a leader and your past doesn't disqualify you. Your past is your past. It is over and done with. It may have been a troubling past, but you were loyal, and people took advantage of it. The Lord says, "Now is the day of your freedom and now is the time for you to be filled with the power and the love of God."

I had never met this man in my life. All of the words slid out of my mouth. I laid hands on him and asked for the Holy Spirit to fill Him. The man stood strong like a statue but then one huge tear fell from his eye. It wasn't a huge dramatic fall out, but I knew he had been touched by the Spirit of God. I turned back to the church and saw the congregation staring intently at the man I just prophesied over. After the meeting was over, I had lunch with the pastors. One of the pastors told me that the third man I had prayed for came from a very troubling past. They told me that the man was once a gang member and was in charge of "eliminating" anyone who opposed the leadership of the gang. The pastor was so excited that the man received that word, because he had been doubting for so long if he belonged to the church and if his sins were too great for him to be loved and used.

That man is called to be a pillar in the church. The devil attempted to take his God-given gifts and use them for his own agenda. The man is called to be a loyal backbone for the church to uphold the integrity of the bride. That is exactly the same role the gang had him doing. The gang had him protect the leadership and to be the strong man to handle any issue that came up. Now, this man is doing exactly what God has created him to do.

Sometime later, I visited the church again. I got to see my friend once again and his heart is on fire for the Lord. I was able to pray for him again, and the power of God swept him off of his feet, and he is also now a small group leader in his church. Your past does not determine if you can encounter the Holy Spirit or not. Saul, before becoming the Apostle Paul, sought to murder and destroy the early Christian Church, my friend had the role of a "hit man" in his early life, and both were consumed with the passion, fire, and love of God. Our sins are not our identity. Are you hungry for Him?

Another time, while on an international trip, we had a tremendous encounter with the Holy Spirit during an impartation meeting. People all over the room were being touched by the love of God and were being set free of many hurts and pains. There were bodies all over the floor. Many times, when people have an encounter with the Holy Spirit, while their spirit is encountering the Holy Spirit, their bodies give out under the power and the glory. They will fall to the ground and the Lord ministers to them. It doesn't hurt and it's not scary. It's quite amazing actually. We were running out of room on the floor for me to pray for people, so I had to move up to the stage to pray for people there. Two young men came forward. I prayed for the first one and he was immediately consumed. My team caught him as he fell out and eased him to the ground. I looked up at the second young man and he looked terrified. You could tell his friend that was laying on the ground possibly conned him into coming and had no idea what was happening. I looked around to take in the sight he was looking at. There were close to a hundred people lying on the ground, other people were on their knees sobbing and praying in tongues, more were dancing and worshiping as the band was in full worship mode, and there I was, a crazy American waving my hand over people and putting them on the ground.

I approached him slowly in the middle of the event and said

very gently, "Hey buddy, how are you?" He stared at me wide eyed and puzzled. "Kind of crazy in here, isn't it?" My question broke some of the tension in his mind. He slightly chuckled and said, "Yes, it is." I leaned in so he could hear me better over all the worship and prayer in the room. "Have you ever seen anything like this before?" He proceeded to tell me no and that he came from a specific conservative church denomination background. I smiled and said, "Bro, that's amazing! I love that denomination. Here, let me explain what all is happening. Do you see your friend on the ground?"

The young man looked down at his friend that I pointed at. He shook his head in agreement. "Your friend was touched by the love and power of God. It's not me doing it, it is God. The Bible says we will receive power when the Holy Spirit comes upon us, and sometimes it is so great, it overwhelms our very being. Your friend will get up in a few moments and he will be a completely changed man. The Holy Spirit is cleansing and empowering him right now to live the life Jesus has called him to. It's not about falling down and crying, it's about your heart and His, colliding."

The young man eased up and shook his head slowly as if saying he understood what I said. "Would you like for me to pray for you? I won't if you don't want me to, I would never force anything on you, and neither will God. You can have it, if you want it." Without hesitation the young man said, "Yes, you can pray." My team gathered behind him and I told him this, "Here is what we are going to do. I want you to know for certain that it is God doing it and not me, so I am going to simply ask God to touch you and I will not put my hand on you. Ok?" The young man nodded in agreement. I smiled and simply prayed, "Lord, touch his heart right now and fill Him with your love, grace, peace, mercy, and power in Jesus name." As I was finishing the prayer the Holy Spirit touched him and he was on the floor praying in a language I had never heard before.

On a funny note, we went for another hour after I prayed for that young man and he never moved a single muscle. He looked like a frozen corpse. One of my ushers came up to me and asked, "Pastor, are you sure he is ok? He looks dead?" I laughed and went over to check on him. The young man laid there peacefully with tears streaming down his face. "He's good buddy." I said to the usher and finished up the meeting. We eventually had to peel the young man off of the floor and help him to his friend's car.

You know, the Bible says, "Don't be drunk on wine, but be filled with the Holy Spirit." This story fits that scripture perfectly. As we peeled the young man off the floor, he was so filled with joy and was boldly declaring his love for Jesus. It was funny and beautiful all at the same time. It doesn't matter what your religious background is. If you grew up in a church that did not ever teach or talk about the Holy Spirit, it doesn't disqualify you from encountering Him. The Holy Spirit isn't just for the charismatic believer, the extraverts, or the "super christian". The Holy Spirit is for everyone. He is for the Baptist, Presbeterian, Catholic, Introvert, the shy, and the uneducated. We have to stop putting the Holy Spirit in a category with certain types of believers. We also have to go beyond the questions of, "What will it look like?" and just simply ask ourselves the question, "Are we hungry for Him?"

Let's talk about kids for a moment. If you have been in the church long enough you may hear this saying, "There is no such thing as a Junior Holy Spirit." What people are saying in that statement is, the Holy Spirit doesn't give a portion of himself to children just because they are young. When a child is filled with the Holy Spirit, they receive ALL of Him. They receive the same portion as an adult does. The Bible even goes to lengths stating adults need to be more childlike in our faith, and Jesus also told His disciples, "Let the children come to me." I think it is imperative to raise our children up in the Lord early. The Bible tells us if we raise our kids up in the ways of the Lord, they will never part from that teaching. I understand why churches have separate services for kids, but I think the content of what is being taught should be as empowering as an adult service. Simply entertaining our kids with bounce houses and funny videos isn't going to prepare our kids for what is ahead for them.

Imagine what it would be like if we taught our children how to hear the voice of God and impart to them the power of the Holy Spirit and raise them up and equip them to understand the fruit of the Spirit and how to walk in their spiritual gifts? The devil wouldn't stand a chance against them as teenagers. My son, who is five at the time of me writing this book, will come up and ask me, "Daddy, do I have the Holy Spirit in me yet?"

I explain it to him this way, "Well, in order for you to have the Holy Spirit in you, you need to accept Jesus as your Lord and Savior, and you will know when the time is right when the Holy Spirit tells you it is time to follow Him."

One time he asked, "How will I know when God is telling me to follow him?" I simply respond with, "One day you will be convicted of the things you do called sin. Sin is doing something Jesus would not do. When conviction comes, you will realize how your sin has separated you from Him and you will have a great desire to want that fixed. Have you had that feeling yet?" His response so far has been, "No, not yet." My son talks about Jesus all the time, we read the Bible together, I teach Him the realities of the Holy Spirit, I share stories with him about signs, wonders, and miracles, and how God has been involved and helping our family, but the most important thing is for him to have his own faith. I'm not being pushy with him or making him say the prayer early so I can feel better about myself. I simply remind him from time to time to ask God to give him conviction and to listen for God's voice to speak into Him.

When my son was at the age of three and four, God used him multiple times to heal me of various things. One time I got a stomach bug and was laying in bed feeling miserable. My son walked in wanting me to go outside and play with him. I told him I couldn't due to my stomach bug and that he should probably stay away from me so he would not get it. Ignoring my warning, my son walked over, pulled my covers down, pulled my shirt up to expose my stomach, he then put his hand on my stomach and said, "Jesus, we thank you for a new tummy, right now in Jesus name. Bug, get out of my daddy right now, in Jesus name." My son then pulled his hand away and said, "Ok daddy, let's go play now."

I was surprised by his bold faith. I honestly didn't quite know how to handle it. I thought for a moment and said, "Let's give Jesus a few minutes to work on my tummy. Why don't you go ahead and start playing and I will catch up with you when I'm all better? Ok?" My son smiles real big and as he ran out of the room he said, "Ok daddy, see you outside in a few minutes." He shut the door and I layed there in the room by myself. My stomach was still rumbling and was just about to start praying to ask God to heal me so my son could know the power of prayer, but before I did, I felt heat in my stomach and all the cramping went away. I laid there for another moment and the heat turned to electricity. A few moments later all the nausea had left and my body felt strong again. Jesus just healed me through the prayer of my son! I jumped out of bed and went outside to see my little boy who had a big smile on his face. I told him I was feeling better and we enjoyed the rest of the day playing together.

I know this story may step on the toes of some people's belief and theology, but that is ok. We need to assume and believe more about who God is and how He can use us to do extraordinary things. My son was between the ages of three and four at this time. He didn't have Bible verses memorized or a theological degree. What he did have was faith. That is what it is all about. Having the confidence in God to take a step out of our own comfort zone and logic and reason to see God move in our own lives or someone else's.

In late 2019, I was asked to be a guest evangelist and participate in a gospel campaign in Nigeria. We went through training under a great Evangelist and were sent out to preach the Gospel in schools during the day and in village outreaches at night leading up to the Great Gospel Crusade that was led by my evangelistic friend. Every morning we would go school to school asking head teachers if we could share with their students. For the most part, teachers were very open and welcoming to us. We would have fifteen minutes to preach the Gospel, lead students and teachers through salvation, and then pray for the filling of the Holy Spirit. Some schools were packed with five year olds, some were high school, and all ages in between. It was a very eye opening experience to see so much happen with so little time. At most of the schools, over ninety percent of the kids and teachers raised their hands to accept Jesus.

I know many people may be thinking, 'Yeah, but did they fully understand what they were getting into? Did you connect them to the church? What if they were just being nice? Did the teachers force them to raise their hands?' I understand if that is your concern, but let me share with you what happened after thousands of these kids prayed to receive Jesus.

After praying, we told them that God wanted to give them a

gift, and that gift is the Holy Spirit. We taught them about the Holy Spirit and how He empowers us to live the life we are called to live and that He gives us power to be a witness. After we taught briefly on the Holy Spirit we would ask the students if they wanted this gift. All of the students would agree and we would ask them to hold out their hands as if receiving a gift and that we were going to ask Jesus to release the Holy Spirit upon them. Let me remind you, this was in the morning, at a school, no lights, no stage, no worship team, and to be fully honest, I wasn't "feeling" the presence of God in most of the quick meetings. We didn't have time to exactly 'prepare' the atmosphere.

We preached a simple and truthful Gospel and the fruit was remarkable. I can't even begin to count how many kids were overwhelmed and filled with the power and love of God. Many kids would become very joyful. Some would cry. Others would shake. There were instances when students began to pray in tongues. Some of our meetings had to go beyond the normal fifteen minutes because the Holy Spirit was moving with such power. Little six year old kids were being filled with the Holy Spirit. Middle school students were being filled. High school students were being filled. And yes, teachers and headmasters were being filled as well. You could not walk away from those meetings and say, "God didn't move." We had far more manifestations of Glory than not. There were even times we had students start manifesting demons and the Lord was so gracious to set them free and fill them with His love.

Age does not matter to the Holy Spirit. Also, the atmosphere doesn't hinder Him either. Many times we think we have to have the mood set for the Holy Spirit. I'm not against powerful worship sets and houses united in prayer, but God wants to move everywhere all the time. You don't have to be "feeling it" for Him to move. It all comes down to hunger. If we are hungry for Him, and desire to know God on a real and personal level, there is nothing that can stop you from encountering Him. Are you hungry for Him?

What more could I say on this topic? I could tell you the story of the time a muslim woman showed up to our event lost and needing directions to get home and not only did she get directions home, but got set free of demonic oppression, saved, and filled with the Holy Spirit. I could tell you about the time we ministered at a student camp where students were not familiar with the filling of the Holy Spirit, but their hunger for Him triggered a mighty wave of glory upon all of their hearts, forever changing many of them. There are countless events of seeing God touch His children and fill their hearts with His goodness and strength without anything limiting Him. Hunger is the key. Jesus said, "Blessed are those who hunger and thirst for righteousness, for they will be filled."

Again, at a festival, Jesus stood up and said, "If anyone is thirsty, come to me and drink. Rivers of living water will flow from their inmost being." The fruit, or evidence, of the Holy Spirit is love, joy, peace, patience, kindness, goodness, faithfulness, gentleness, and self-control. The only way we can change is by encountering the unchanging love and heart of God. We don't ever need to become timid of what God desires to give us. He desires to give us His heart, and the way He chose to do that is by giving us His Spirit. Also, encountering the Holy Spirit is not just a one time thing. We are constantly going through changes and levels of sanctification. In order to change we have to have an ongoing experience and encounter with Him. The only question you need to ask yourself is, are you hungry for Him?

Jesus, I want to know you more. I ask that you fill me with the power and love of the Holy Spirit. Help me become more hungry for your presence every day. Teach me how to be more sensitive to your presence. Fill me with your love, joy, and peace. Release the teacher, helper, and comforter into my life so that I may be empowered to live the life you have called me to live and to be a witness of your goodness and grace. Jesus, I surrender every area of my heart to you. Come Holy Spirit, come.

TWELVE

Unity in the Bride

I do not ask for these only, but also for those who
will believe in me through their word, that
they may all be one, just as you, Father, are
in me, and I in you, that they also may be in
us, so that the world may believe that you
have sent me. John 17:20-21

WHAT IS it you hope the most for yourself? What do you want to see Jesus do in your life this very moment? What is your hope for government, education, business, sports, media, entertainment, families, and the Church of the nation you live in? How could you see God restoring these aspects of society and how can you imagine God using you to be a part of the restoration and revival? Do you ever think of what it will be like when you stand face to face with Jesus? Do you ponder about what Heaven will look like and what Jesus might say to you? Will the people you told about Jesus be there with you? These are a few of the many questions I think about often. Many times, at the end of the day, I will reflect back on the decisions I made and my actions to determine if I was trying to glorify Jesus during the day, or just promote my own name. I believe God is getting His Bride prepared for the Bridegroom, Jesus. I believe we are stepping into a time where the Church is going to start operating in the passion, authority, and love she is called into.

Years ago, I heard the Lord tell me He was going to cleanse the United States of the spirit of mediocrity. There would be a point at which our country would have a left and a right, but no middle (not implying political left and right, but we are seeing that as well). Another way to say it is black and white, without the gray. You could also say hot and cold, but no more lukewarm. It seems in these days we are living in, we know exactly what everyone thinks and how firm they are on their opinions and beliefs. We now see that our country is at polar opposites with each other on many things. In the eyes of the world we could look at the condition of our country and think it is an absolute disaster, but really, I think a bold line in the sand had to be drawn for comparison. If people don't know where they stand, they don't know how far or how indifferent they are from the truth. I believe Jesus has drowned out the spirit of mediocrity in this nation to prepare for a move of God like we have never seen before. Honestly, it is already happening. With all the opposition the United States has been in, people are discovering what they have been fighting for or standing for isn't bringing them fulfillment. We are seeing in the Church all over the world, people are tired of watered down preaching. Because of the bold stance of wickedness, righteousness is rising up to the occasion. As I write this chapter, I am sitting in my backyard, in beautiful Texas, at night, next to a campfire. All around me is darkness, except for the intense glow of the flames. If it were in the middle of the day, the flames would not be as bright and wouldn't stand out as much. So it is the same for this hour in our Nation. The Kingdom of darkness is in full attack, but the more the enemy tries, the more our light shines greater.

I also believe we are in the time of a Saul to David transition. By God's grace, He is convicting leaders to not just be obedient to a few things but to be surrendered fully in all things. He is giving them time to change the direction of their hearts so they can fulfill their destiny He has given them. I believe many leaders in the world will turn around and run full hearted after Jesus once again, for those who are too tired to carry on and not want to change their ways, God has prepared a generation of mighty ones that are ready to lay their entire lives down at a moments notice for the sake of the cross. I believe these newly empowered leaders will have a great value for the tenacity in the young generation, and give great honor and respect for the maturity and experience of our more seasoned generations. I also believe these leaders will bring unity between the Conservative and Charismatic Church.

It seems as if there was a divorce in the church along with a custody battle. We have on one side the Conservative Church and the Charismatic on the other. Oftentimes you may hear a Baptist make a joke about the Pentecostals or hear an Assembly of God member make a comment about a Presbyterian. How did we get to this underlying tone of separation and indifference? Just for the record, I have great respect for both sides. I think they are both extremely important for the Body of Christ. I will explain why I think that later in this chapter. It seems we have this great divide in the church, but it doesn't stop there. There are common themes and values you see and hear on both sides. The conservatives have a high value for doctrine and community. Nobody can do community like the Baptists! But, when the spirit of religion creeps into the Conservative Church they are likely to replace the Holy Spirit with the Bible alone, and instead of a relationship with the Spirit, they pick a relationship with each other. Of course, both the Bible and relationship with people are not bad things, but the Bible is to point us to having a deeper relationship with the Father, through Jesus, in the Holy Spirit. It wasn't intended to REPLACE the Holy Spirit.

The Charismatic Church is of course big on spiritual gifts and the Holy Spirit. If you want a Holy Ghost party, you go to the Charismatics! But, when the spirit of religion creeps into the Charismatic Church they are likely to replace doctrine for feelings, and gifts for position and recognition. I've had individuals tell me, "I don't need the Bible, I have the Holy Spirit." If my jaw could hit the floor it would in those moments. It is dangerous to replace the Word and the Spirit in place of the other. They are meant to complement one another, not replace. Trust me, there is a reason why I am saying all of this. I'm not saying it to try and bring division. There already is division. We have to discuss why there is division so we can solve the issue and get the church back in her rightful place. Plus, it is a good thing to be aware of potential weaknesses. I used to teach my martial art students all the time what their strengths and weaknesses were. I would teach them those things so that they could be aware.

Our enemy knows what our weaknesses are and will always try to take us out by exploiting them. If we can recognize it and fortify it before the enemy attacks, we have a much stronger chance of being successful. It's the same with the five fold ministry. I know as an evangelist, my greatest strength is my passion, but if I ever allow my passion to become worldly, it could hurt me. Pastors are great shepherds, but if their giftings become earthly they can become controlling. Teachers are great about diving into the depths of God's Word, but they have to be careful not to become overly analytical. Prophets are great about hearing God, but if offense gets in their hearts, they can be condemning rather than life-giving. Apostles are amazing builders but if their gifts become of the world, they can tear down in seconds what took them years to build. I think it is important to know these things about ourselves so we can stay alert and vigilant against such things.

So let me get back to my point. As I was saying earlier, it seems we have had a divorce and custody battle in the church. We have the conservative side that has doctrine and community and the charismatics with the Holy Spirit and the gifts. Here is what I believe the Lord has been showing me in the past year. God wants to bring unity between the two. This is what I heard Him say to me one night, "Son, you can't have revival without the Holy Spirit, and you cannot sustain it without community."

Let's think about this for a moment. How often do we see the fires of revival ignite to see the flame quickly burn out in the hearts of believers. All over the world, it seems the church is having a new revival every other weekend somewhere. I'm not against these things, revival is awesome, but it should be much easier sustaining and fire rather than having to restart one.

I believe the devil understands this and that is why he has tried so hard to put a wedge between the two sides of the church. We need each other. We need to see the value and strengths of each other, because you cannot have good doctrine without the Holy Spirit, and you cannot fully understand the Holy Spirit without good doctrine. Spiritual gifts are not as effective without community, and community is not effective without spiritual gifts. We have to rise above the non essentials debates and start valuing each other. Am I saying the denominations should become one?

Absolutely not. All I am saying is, I believe God wants The Church to be united under His love and covering and that we value each other for the different gifts we have. I believe in the days to come we will see more and more of this unity.

You may be asking, "That sounds great Dennis, but what role do I play in this?" I ask myself that question all the time. The answer is simple, relationships. It may not be our role to get church leaders to get along with one another, but we can have a say so in who we get along with. We should make friends with people of different denominations. We share with them our passions and desire for unity and let love bring the correct doctrine to light.

False doctrine cannot survive when love is present. Love exposes every false belief because it cannot produce fruit like love can. Scripture says, "You will know a tree by its fruit." Love is like a purifying fire and false doctrines cannot survive it. Whatever is true will remain after the fire of love. That is also why I believe Jesus said the two greatest commandments were, "Love the Lord your God with all of your heart, soul, mind, and strength, and the second is like the first, love your neighbor as yourself." Scriptures also say, "God is love."

Well, if scriptures are a direct representation of who God is, then would true and authentic love that comes from God expose who He is and who He is not? We need to understand that we are living in very exciting times. We were not put here to just be church attenders, but to be the actual Church, and it is our calling and our privilege to destroy hell in people's lives and usher in Heaven.

Jesus, I pray You use me to bring unity to your bride, the Church.
Lord, if there is any bitterness in my heart towards another believer,

please show me, so that I may repent and be free from the bondage that comes from it. Jesus, I pray for the leaders in my nation. I pray that they hear your voice and fall in love with you. Holy Spirit, empower me to seek unity and peace with everyone I meet. Teach me how to see the best in others, rather than what is wrong. Lord, I pray for the removal of any wedge or hindrance that may be separating Churches from uniting. Your word says you will be returning for a spotless bride, without wrinkle or blemish. Cleanse me, empower me, and use me to prepare the Church to be a unified bride for you.

In Jesus name I pray. Amen.

THIRTEEN

30, 60, or 100 fold?

*"Still other seed fell on good soil, where it
    produced a crop - a hundred, sixty, or thirty
    times what was sown. Whoever has ears, let
    them hear."*
Matthew 13:8-9

"WELL, WHICH ONE ARE YOU?" I heard the Lord ask me as I was
reading the parable of the sower in Matthew, Chapter 13. In this
parable, Jesus is painting a picture of what happens when people
hear the Gospel.

He says some people, when they hear it, they will not understand it, and the enemy will come and snatch what little understanding they have away from them. There are other people that
will receive the Good News of the Gospel, but when trouble
comes, they fall away. There will also be people who will hear the
Gospel but allow the worries of life and the deceitfulness of

wealth to suffocate what little belief they have, making them unfruitful. Then, Jesus talks about another kind of people, a people who hear the Word, understand it, and are obedient to it. These amazing people will produce incredible fruit for Jesus. Some of them will produce thirty times what was given to them, others will produce sixty times as much, and then there are the mighty ones that will produce what is known as a hundred fold, which actually means, immeasurably more.

I like to try and grasp with my thoughts what it will be like to stand face to face with Jesus in Heaven when I have finished this life on earth. I try to imagine the intense love in His eyes, His smile, How His voice will shake my inmost being, the joy that radiates from Him, the way He walks, His laugh, and what it will feel like to hug Him. There was a period of time when I would think of such things, I would have another thought barge in and interrupt, and that thought was, am I living this life the way Jesus has destined me to? Will I stand before Him and hear Him say, "Well done, My good and faithful servant?" Or will I allow the troubles of life keep me in a lower form of being and hear Him say, "I had planned for you and I to do so much more together while you were down there on earth, but you allowed hurts, pains, and false opinions to hold you back rather than letting me heal you?" I used to find myself anxious while deep in thought, worried I didn't have what it takes to live the life He has called me to live or that my calling was smaller than my desires. I would have the biggest dreams in my heart and I would hear something tell me, "You can't dream that big, you will never do anything that great. Dreams like that are for 'special' Christians, not you. Be happy with smaller dreams. You are being selfish." It is a very bizarre thing to mistake the devil's voice for God's. I thought for years that God was telling me those things. I thought it was Him telling me not to get my hopes up too much and that I should settle for less. I would sometimes hear the phrase, "Stop thinking you are a hundred fold kind of guy. You are lucky if you make it to thirty fold." As I type these things out and as I read them, I realize how ridiculous it was for me to believe it was God who told me these things. That's how the enemy works though. He chips away at us with a small lie and then another until, many small lies turn into a huge catastrophe of an identity crisis. I have also learned that I am not the only person in the world the enemy comes after and tries to convince believers that God wants less for someone rather than more. Let's spend some time confronting the enemy's lies and discover the truth.

I have been teaching my five-year-old son about the Gospel. I try to use different illustrations to teach him the realities of Heaven and who God is. The most recent illustration I had for him involved four solo cups. I labeled the cups, Father, Jesus, Holy Spirit, and You. I started out by teaching him about the Trinity and the Gospel story. After that, I wanted to teach him something that took quite some time for me to understand. I took the Jesus cup and the cup that said You on it. I asked my son, "What did Jesus do for you?"

My son quickly said, "Jesus is the Son of God, who loves me, and died for my sin!" I responded back with, "That's exactly right, but did He stay dead?" My son jumped up off the ground and with a serious voice, "No Dad, He didn't. He's alive and in Heaven."

I laughed and said, "You nailed it buddy. Here is something new I want to teach you." He got really excited and sat back on the ground with me. "Do you know the Bible says when we give our lives to Jesus that we are put IN CHRIST?" His puzzled look made me laugh. "IN JESUS?" He asked, trying to connect the dots. "Yes, our lives are now in His, So, if YOU are in JESUS, how would you show me that with your cups?" My son thought for a minute and picked up the cup that said YOU and stacked it inside the Jesus cup. He pulled his hands away and looked at me eager to know if he had done it right.

"Bro, you are on fire today. You did that perfectly. Let me ask you something, can you see the cup that says You on it?" He looked at me as if I were trying to trick him. "No." He finally said with hesitation. "I can only see the 'Jesus' cup."

"Exactly" I exclaimed. "Do you know that when our Father in Heaven looks at you, He sees you the same way He sees Jesus?" My son stared at me and then back at the cups. "Daddy, God looks at me the same way He looks at Jesus?"

"Yes sir. When we belong to Jesus, He views us the same way He views Jesus. How amazing is that?" I asked him.

His smile got really big and said, "I want to be in Jesus." It was an awesome time.

I think there are many Christians in the world that are having a hard time grasping what it is to be in Christ. When our Father in Heaven looks at us, He sees us through the lens of Jesus. That means when He is looking at us He only sees what is right about us (what matches Jesus) and what is missing (what we haven't received yet). That is the whole point of conviction. The Holy Spirit convicts us of the things we are missing, not to condemn us, but to invite us into an encounter with God to receive more of who Jesus is, so that we can become more of who we are called to be.

I want my children to know what it means to be the Beloved of Christ and I want the same thing for you. Jesus didn't just die and was raised from the dead to get us into Heaven, He did those things to set us free from an empty way of living. Meaning, our lives are to be filled with purpose and destiny, to be consumed with the Glory of God, to radiate His goodness and favor everywhere we go, and to redeem the time in the present darkness this world is living in.

We have been given the Spirit of a limitless God who has a raging fire of love and compassion for you and me. Our greatest dreams do not even come close to His kind intentions and the desires He has for us. I guess what I am trying to say is, God wants to use us to do greater things than we could possibly ever imagine and He knew in order to do that, He needed to put us someplace safe where we could grow, develop, mature, and be empowered, and that is IN CHRIST. When we come to understand this we become better at discerning the spiritual voices speaking to us. We then know that any voice that tries to down size us, down play our gifts and desires, attempt to make us feel less-than, is the enemy.

Did you know that Satan is depressed? That he has anxiety attacks all the time? Did you know that he is angry, bitter, upset, scared, insecure and prideful at the same time, poor, broken, desperate, and lustful? Whenever Satan starts to accuse you of these things, just remember, he is only talking about himself while using your name. Christians are not called to inherit Heaven and spend their lives thinking like Hell. For those the Son sets free, is free indeed.

So, what are we to do with this freedom? What do we do with this outrageous love we have been given? Live a partial life of obedience? Live a good enough life where the good things we do outweigh the bad? Attempt to be a good employee where we work, not ruin our marriage, make sure our kids are not heathens, and try to attend church every once and awhile? Or, are we to produce a hundred fold for Jesus, tearing down every demonic strategy we encounter and release the Kingdom of God into every situation and person we come across by loving everyone the same way Jesus loves us? What will you do with all of this beautiful freedom Jesus has given you? It's a big question to answer. What if God is His children in this hour, "Which one are you? 30, 60, or 100 fold for Me?"

The day He asked me that question I was sitting in my usual place, thinking it was an ordinary day, not prepared to have such an encounter. I had just read the parable of the sower and wasn't feeling super spiritual to be fully honest with you.

I was about to carry on reading when His voice stilled my heart asking, "Well, which one are you?" It surprised me how clear His voice was in the moment.

"Which one of what, Lord?" I asked not relating His voice to the scripture I just read.

"Son, which one are you going to be for Me? Are you going to produce 30, 60, or 100 fold for me?"

I sat in silence for what felt like minutes. I was confused, "You mean, I get to pick, Lord?" For some reason, I had always thought God was the one who picked who produced 30, 60, or 100 fold. I had always connected that belief to the verse, "We are God's handiwork, created in Christ Jesus to do good works, which He planned in advance for us to do." I was convinced He chose and now He is asking me which one I am?

"Of course you get to pick, son! If it were up to Me, everyone would produce 100 fold!" That statement overwhelmed me. It is God's intention and desire for every single person to produce a hundred fold for His Kingdom. To bear much fruit, to reach multitudes of lost people for Him, to live a life full of signs, wonders, and miracles, to be found trustworthy with some and be given much. I instantly knew how I wanted to answer Him, but I was afraid. I knew my spirit was on board, but my soul was still at war with myself. "Do I have to give you an answer right now?" I asked Him.

"No, I'll wait." I could feel HIs cheerful tone but could also feel how serious He was about me answering this question.

I wish I could tell you I answered Him ten minutes later and everything was great, but that would be a lie. I didn't answer the question for two weeks and I never told anyone. I would even try to talk to the Lord about other things hoping He would maybe give me a pass on the question and carry on as if it didn't matter. I would ask the Lord something and it would be complete silence. I tried it for days. I could feel Him but He was not going to let this one slide. "You really want me to answer this question, don't you?" I asked.

"Yes son, it is very important."

A few more days went by and I was wrestling with myself. Why was I having so much trouble with this? Why couldn't I just answer God with what my spirit wanted to and move on?

I finally realized what the problem was. I didn't see myself the way He was seeing Me. He was seeing me through the lens of Jesus and with Jesus, there are no boundaries, limits, weaknesses, or restrictions. It's just Him, and He is everything. I was looking at myself and trying to measure myself up to the question. I was considering my own boundaries, limits, weaknesses, and restrictions. I had made the question more about me than about Jesus.

I spent a few more days praying into this new revelation and clarity that He was gracious enough to show me. Finally, the day came. I went and sat in the place I like to go when I want to hang out with God. I became still and aware of His presence. "Lord?" I said out loud, "I have an answer for you!" I instantly felt His delight draw up in my heart. It felt as if He was gazing deeper into me than ever before.

"What will it be, son?" He asked.

I began to have tears roll down my cheeks knowing that what I was about to say was going to change many things in my life. "I decide, right now, that I am going to produce a hundred fold for you. This is what I want. I want my life to be a life You have full reign and control over, without limits or restrictions."

His presence and peace in the room was so tangible. It's hard to explain, but there are times you can actually feel how God is feeling in a moment. I instantly felt this overwhelming joy rise up inside of me and I could feel His excitement growing.

"There you go, son. I knew you could do it."

I sat there wiping tears from my eyes and I asked Him this question, "Lord, How do I handle this? What do I do with this decision? Are there some things I need to give you or any changes I need to make?"

The Lord responded with a statement that brought new light and clarity to His Word, heart, and intentions. He said, "You now know how to govern your life."

In this life we will make millions of decisions on what we will do and how we will do it. It can be easy to get caught up in all the wrong things and miss out on all of the purposeful ones. I knew in that moment I finally had a measure to help me in life determine what was good for me to do and what was not.

Every potential action and response in my life is now measured to the question, "Will this action or response lead to producing a hundred fold?" If I have peace about it and I believe it will be fruitful, I do it. If I don't feel peace or that the response or action glorifies me more than it does Him, I'm not budging. When we come to the decision of what kind of life we are going to live for

Jesus, we are empowered to function in that capacity. We have to be willing to live a life outside of our own comfort zone to see faith manifest fruit that will advance the Kingdom of God! This is not a name it and claim it kind of decision. It is a heartfelt covenant with the Lord. It is a declaration and decision to give Jesus your all. To give Him your undivided heart without conditions. The world is awaiting to see a people who have an undivided and completely sold out heart for King Jesus. A people that don't rely on their own strength or earthly knowledge, but a people who know what it means to be in Christ and to have His fullness dwell within them. Jesus didn't withhold any part of Himself for us. It is the least we can do to not withhold any part of ourselves to Him.

The only thing we ever have to give up for Jesus is the identity of someone we never were in the first place. We have the opportunity to walk away from what hinders us to embrace all that He is, and when we embrace all that He is, we understand the real us.

So, which one are you? What will you produce for God? 30, 60, or 100 fold? Remember, both God and Satan want to use your past. Satan wants to use your past to remind you of your failures and keep you in a lower form of being to keep you from inheriting all that God has for you. God wants to use your past as a weapon and permission to go and set others free from the very same thing that once had you in bondage.

Yesterday's failures are tomorrow's permission. What you failed at in your past, you now have permission to liberate people from. Let your opinion of yourself be determined by Jesus, and no one or nothing else. Jesus has made up His mind about us. It is time we do the same.

Jesus, I want to worship and honor You in everything I do. Please teach me and show me how to live a life that produces a hundred fold for the Kingdom of God. Allow my thoughts to be your thoughts, so that I may know how to govern my life the way you want. Let your love increase in my heart and let the influences of the world decrease. Jesus, give me the ability to be able to quickly recognize your voice and teach me how to become deaf to the enemy's lies. In Jesus' name I pray. Amen.

FOURTEEN

Umbrellas and Waterfalls

He must become greater; I must become
less.
John 3:30

A MAN STANDS on a rock in a raging river. He's shaking, but he is
not cold. His eyes are wide with astonishment, His hair is blown
back by the force in front of him, and his hand is cramping by
tightly holding a black umbrella that is shielding him from what
he is face to face with. The man on the river stands in front of a
raging waterfall. Millions of gallons of water crash in front of him
per second. The man attempts to grasp how great this waterfall
actually is. He looks to his left and then looks to his right and realizes he can't see where the waterfall ends. He looks up and all he
sees is water crashing down. He attempts to find the sky but is
unable to locate where this great waterfall ends and where the sky
begins.

He feels like an ant standing at the face of Niagara Falls. The waterfall roars with such intensity that it shakes his very soul. You would think that a man would be trembling in fear, but there is something different about this waterfall. The man feels drawn to it. It is as if the waterfall is inviting him in. He feels the pull of the raging abyss but then backs away and tightens his grip even more on the black umbrella. Suddenly, the man hears a voice from behind him. The voice is as gentle as a whisper, but yet made the waterfall sound like a water faucet. "Well, aren't you going to get in?"

The man turned quickly to see who spoke with such power and peace. Astonished and amazed, the man sees the one who spoke. A man walking on the water heading straight towards him. The man with the black umbrella can see the holes in the man's hands, the holes in his feet, eyes with more intensity than the waterfall, and a smile that radiated like the sun... It was Jesus. "Do you like your waterfall?" Jesus asked the man with the black umbrella.

The man turned and looked back at the eternal waterfall and then back to Jesus, "My waterfall?" He asked timidly. "Yes, of course." Jesus said, as He now stood side by side with the man clinching the black umbrella. "I made this waterfall just for you." Confused by Jesus' statement, he asks, "Why do you want me to get in?" Jesus laughs with joy and puts his arm around the man as He addresses the question while admiring the waterfall, "When you step into this waterfall, everything in your life will change. Every part of your being will spring to life and you will become all the things I desire for you to be... and you will also become the person you have always wanted to be." The man looks at Jesus and then studies the waterfall again. "So, do I just walk in?" He asks. "Yes, just walk in. You don't have to do anything to earn your way into this waterfall, just walk in."

"Jesus, I'm not comfortable stepping into this thing without knowing what it is. How is this waterfall going to change me? What is so special about it?" The man asks as he clings even tighter to his black umbrella. Jesus turns with sincerity towards the man, "Son, this waterfall is my love for you." The man was prepared for many answers, expect that one. After studying the waterfall a little bit more, he takes a deep breath, grabs his black umbrella with both hands, and steps into the waterfall. Immediately, he is engulfed by a sea of falling water and he makes himself as small as he can under the shelter of his umbrella. The man turns in the waterfall back towards Jesus. He waits for all the changes to come that Jesus promised him, but nothing happened. He's in the waterfall and water is pouring off of his umbrella, but he remains dry.

"Jesus, why am I not changing? You said I would change?" The man shouts in protest. Jesus walks closer to the frustrated man and points to the umbrella. "Son, give me the umbrella." Shocked that Jesus said that he immediately responds, "No Jesus, I can't give you this umbrella. I've always had this umbrella. I don't know what I would do if I didn't have this umbrella!"

"I know what you would do without the umbrella." Jesus said.

"What? What could I possibly do without this umbrella that I have had since I can remember?" The man screamed from within the waterfall.

Jesus stares for a moment and then responds, "Everything. You can do everything."

"What do you mean, Jesus?" tears rolled down the man's eyes.

"Son, you are still hanging onto many hurts and pains. That umbrella is not there to protect you, it is there to hinder you. I know the hurts, pains, and struggles in your life. I know the shame you carry from those who have hurt you. I know the disappointments you have faced day in and day out. But, even though you have struggled and have held onto so many things, I still love you. My love for you has never changed. This love has always been here for you. There is only one thing that has changed, and that is your ability to receive my love. Right now you are standing in my love, but because of the hurts and the pain you still choose to hold onto, you haven't received it yet. Son, please, give Me the umbrella." Jesus holds out his hand and the man sees the hole in Jesus' palm.

The man realizes he has used the umbrella to be a crutch and a defense mechanism his entire life. He takes one final look at the umbrella and then sets his attention to Jesus. Finally, letting go of past failures, resentments, struggles, and grudges, he hands the umbrella to Jesus and is completely hidden in the waterfall that Jesus made just for him.

The story I shared with you was from a dream I had years ago. It was a very liberating and humbling moment at the same time. I love how the Lord corrects us. He does it with a sincere love with unfiltered truth, while maintaining a joy that is contagious. There really is a measure of love that is set aside for each and every single one of us. Even the people who don't choose to follow Jesus still have a waterfall of love ready for them. It is up to them if they will receive it or not. God doesn't turn on the waterfall when someone says, 'yes.' His love has been there for us long before we were even born. We just have to decide to jump in, without reserve or partial ownership. The umbrella in the story can represent many different things for a believer. It can be bitterness, unforgiveness, sin, pride, insecurity, disappointment, shame, curses, doubts, fears, and many more. The beautiful thing is, we don't have to keep it. Whatever we are struggling with, we can totally surrender to Him and move on from our lives purified and empowered. As

Christians, we no longer have a sin 'nature', just a sin 'habit.' The Bible says we are a new creation in Christ Jesus, not an upgraded version of our broken selves. So that means our former selves died, and when that version of 'you' died, so did its nature. Now, all that remains is a habit that your soul (mind, will, and emotions) have become familiar with. We have to be a people that make our souls surrender to the ways of the spirit so our flesh will become obedient to the new way of life we are called to live. The best way to accomplish this is by putting our focus on the waterfall rather than the umbrella.

I want to share this prophetic word with you. I believe this word is for many different people whom He is calling and drawing to Himself. If you feel like life has been heavy, you are burdened with many things, you are longing for His presence, or are facing sickness, disease, or guilt; this prophetic encouragement is for you.

"Beloved, no matter what you're feeling right now in this moment. No matter what hurts or secrets you are hiding, I am here. I am here for you and I'm not here to embarrass you, shame you, or ridicule you, but to rescue you. I know what you have faced and the struggles that lie so deep within. I know the despair that comes knocking on your door at night and the grief that looms around the corner. I know what darkness haunts your thoughts and dreams. I know them all. I know the conflict in your mind about Me, I know the lies that have been whispered to you for so long, and I know the heaviness that's on your shoulders, the anxiety in your breath, and the passion that you have been robbed of. My love, I know them all.

That is why I am here. I am here with you right now, and the reason that I'm here is to show you. Not just tell you but show you My love that I have for you. The day of searching it is over. I am what you seek. I am the hope and joy and the longing of your heart. I am the one who puts breath into you. I am He that loves you outrageously and I need you to know that. Right now, I need you to know that I love you just as you are. You do not have to earn this love that I have for you. I cannot love you any less or any more than I do right now. My love is a complete love. My love is set and it cannot be overturned or manipulated. It cannot be surpassed and it will never ever change. For my love is perfect for you and I want you to have it.

There is enough of me to go around for all of eternity. I love you in a way that brings life to dead hearts. It brings joy to the depressed. My love brings peace to the troubled and patience to the anxious. My love is so amazing for you that it will overwhelm you with a sense of kindness that will drive away all bitterness in your soul. The darkness I know you've been victim of will be overwhelmed by the goodness of my love, and my love is so faithful and it is so contagious it will fill your heart with faithfulness, and when the spirit of my love comes upon you, it will rapidly grow a character of self control like you have never imagined.

My love for you is eternal and it does not lack in any way. I want you to have it. I want you to have it all. I want you to come to a place where you can receive it all. It is fully available right here and right now. Make me number one love of your life and you can have it all. All you have to give up is everything you were never intended to be. What I'm saying is, you don't have to be anything that you're not. Hey, the mask can come off now. You don't need to hide. I love the real you. I take such great pleasure in the real you. I adore who you're created to be.

So, right now you can have it all. You can have all of Me. You can have my love. You can have peace and security. You can have the healing that I paid for. You can have the freedom from the pain that I conquered on the cross. You can also have My Spirit as a down payment. It's all here for you. Come to me all of you who are weary, all of you are burdened, and I will give you rest. For those who have been carrying the burden of life on your shoulders, give it to Me. I'll trade you for mine! It's amazingly light.

Bring your sicknesses and diseases before me, I'll take care of it for you. Give me the failures of your past and the fear of tomorrow and I'll make right now amazing. Bring your rejections, your low self esteem, and your self-hatred and I will give you acceptance, faith, and identity. This is the good news. This is who I am. I want you to have me and never ever lack again. You have to understand that I cannot force this on you. I cannot force my love. You have to decide and call out. I'm like a man knocking on a door! Will you let me in? Will you let me love you, heal you, and free and fill your heart with everything that I am?"

YOU MAY BE ASKING YOURSELF, "Ok Dennis, I just read the prophetic word and this is the final chapter of the book.... so, what do I do with all of this? How do I respond? What are you suggesting I do with all of this information?" Those are great questions to ask and I would answer your questions with this simple response, "Choose the voice of Life." Throughout your life and even now, you have been hearing two different voices. One voice tells you in life, "Walk away. You can't have it. It's not for you. You are not good enough." And the second voice says, "Come to Me. You CAN have Me. I made it all available. You were worth dying for." As you can probably tell, the first voice is demonic and the second is Jesus. Anytime we are exposed to the truth and the kind intentions of our Lord and Savior, we have to make a choice. We will either choose to walk away or run towards. The enemy will always try very hard to keep a believer from fully believing, but whenever we decide to choose the voice of Life that is speaking into our hearts, the voice of the enemy gets quieter and quieter.

What if today is the day you choose to run towards God's heart? What if today was the day you put away the struggles, ignored the lies, forgave those who hurt you, renounced the false opinions, and just simply said yes to Jesus? What if today is the day when you go from partial surrender to full surrender? Imagine what would change in your life, in your family's life, in your future! It's all ready and available! Remember, you don't have to be anything you are not, and walking away from the things that have hurt you is giving up things you were never intended to have in the first place. You lose nothing and gain everything. If you have been following Jesus for many years, let your fire grow even more in this moment. If you are a believer and feel like your love has gone cold, ask for a fresh impartation of His Spirit. He will come and set your heart ablaze again. If you feel like you don't have a relationship with Jesus or know you don't, let's take care of that. We are never supposed to spend our lives as Christians 'hoping' we are saved. We are supposed to 'know' we are saved. We go from hoping to knowing by giving our lives to Jesus and allowing Him to fill us with His Spirit. If you want to go from 'hoping' you're saved to 'knowing,' go to the end of the book and read the salvation prayer out loud. If you say that prayer with faith and a sincere heart, your life will change forever.

So, my final advice for you is to go all in. Take everything you have read and make it your own. Jesus has a beautiful and unique calling on your life. Just because you may not be in "ministry" doesn't mean God can't use you. He delights in using ALL of His children. But, before considering how He might want to work through you, fall in love with what He wants to do in you. Seek His presence and His voice daily. Allow Jesus to be your number one fascination for the rest of your life. When you read your Bible and don't know which theology or belief to pick, choose the theology that makes Jesus more and man less. John the Baptist said, "He must become greater and I must become less." In a world that will try to tell you, over and over again, that Jesus isn't who the Bible says He is, don't lose heart. Smile, love people, and be the light of the world, because you know through your beautiful relationship with God, Jesus is still Jesus.

Salvation Prayer

"*Jesus,*

I believe in You. I believe you are the Son of God. I believe that you died for my sins and rose from the grave victorious. Jesus, I have sin in my life, and I need your forgiveness. Please, forgive me of my sins and remove any stronghold the devil may have over my life. I forgive those who have hurt me, and I forgive myself for mistakes I have made. Jesus, I ask that you save me and fill me with your Holy Spirit right now. Thank you, Jesus, for loving me and saving me. I declare that I am all yours and you are all mine.

In Jesus name,
Amen."

About Five Crowns

WE ARE DRIVEN AND PASSIONATE TO SEE THE CHURCH BE THE CHURCH

"It is our desire and calling to Advance the Gospel, Empower the Believers, and Unite the Church. Everyone in the world needs to hear the Good News of Jesus, and Five Crowns is taking the message to them. Along with that, we are driven and passionate to see the Church be the Church. We are called to be empowered and united. We believe God has put us on a journey to speak life and encouragement into God's children and to see denominations united. We can not have revival without the Holy Spirit and we can not sustain it without community. We know that when we are empowered and united, we will see the greatest revival this world has ever seen."

-Dennis Funderburg Jr.

CEO of Five Crowns

01. Advance the Gospel

Five Crowns number one priority is to carry out the calling that Jesus gave the church to advance the gospel. In Matthew 28:18-20 Jesus says, "All authority in heaven and on earth has been given to me. Go therefore and make disciples of all nations, baptizing them in the name of the Father, and of the Son and of the Holy Spirit, teaching them to observe all that I have commanded you. And behold, I am with you always, to the end of the age."(ESV)

02. Empower the Believers

Five Crowns actively works to equip and empower believers. In Ephesians 4:11-13 it says, "So Christ himself gave the apostles, the prophets, the evangelists, the pastors and teachers, 12 to equip his people for works of service, so that the body of Christ may be built up 13 until we all reach unity in the faith and in the knowledge of the Son of God and become mature, attaining to the whole measure of the fullness of Christ." The desire of Five Crowns is that believers would become mature and empowered with the whole measure of the fullness of Christ.

03. Unite the Church

The heart of Five Crowns to unite the church comes straight from the heart of Jesus. That in Him believers would act as one body. In John 17:20-20-23 Jesus prays, "My prayer is not for them alone. I pray also for those who will believe in me through their message, 21 that all of them may be one, Father, just as you are in me and I am in you. May they also be in us so that the world may believe that you have sent me. 22 I have given them the glory that you gave me, that they may be one as we are one— 23 I in them and you in me—so that they may be brought to complete unity.

Then the world will know that you sent me and have loved them even as you have loved me."(NIV)

Five Crowns International Ministries
    P.O. Box 1707
    Granbury, Texas 76048

Learn more at https://5crowns.org/

About the Author

Dennis is the founder of Five Crowns International Ministries. He is married to his high school sweetheart, Miranda, and have two amazing children. Dennis grew up in a small Texas town and was a martial arts instructor and competitor. In October of 2011, Dennis encountered Jesus in the middle of the night that changed his life forever. When starting his journey in ministry, Dennis served in children's ministry and then progressed his way through student ministry, counseling, and was a campus pastor at Stone-Water Church. After six and a half years of service in the local Church, Dennis responded to God's call to take a leap of faith into going full time in Five Crowns.

Dennis travels all over the world preaching the Gospel of Jesus. His goal is to see millions of people get saved, healed, and delivered in his lifetime and for the Five Crowns ministry to continue to be a ministry that empowers believers and bring unity to the Church until Jesus' return. Dennis is the author of the Jesus is still Jesus book and is the host for the Jesus is still Jesus podcast.

CPSIA information can be obtained
at www.ICGtesting.com
Printed in the USA
BVHW010038131021
618745BV00001B/1